THROUGH MY CAT'S EYES

A Year in the Life of a Colorado Mountain Cat

TROY JONES

Copyright © 2017 by Troy Jones

All rights reserved.

No part of this book may be reproduced in any form or by any electronic or mechanical means, including information storage and retrieval systems, without written permission from the author, except for the use of brief quotations in a book review.

CONTENTS

1. The Abandonment	1
2. The Great Adoption	9
3. The Long Winter	35
4. The Big Rabbit	49
5. Winter Varmints	55
6. The New Year	61
7. The Bond at Castle Ridge	71
8. The Endless Summer	85
9. Mice in the House	105
10. Dr. Lemmons	117
11. No Diesel Trucks	123
12. First of Nine Lives	131
13. The Vanishing Act	137
14. Proof of Telepathy	143
15. The Cat, the Bat, and the Snake	147
16. Big Dogs	153
17. Buena Vista	161
18. The Growl	173
19. My Special Dad	183
Afterword	187
Also by Troy Jones	189
Acknowledgments	191
About the Author	193

Chapter One
THE ABANDONMENT

Note: To enjoy the book's photos in full color, check out Lucky's website: https://luckyswebsite.weebly.com/

I was born in the mountains near Buena Vista, Colorado. I am a grey and black striped tiger cat with a white chest and paws. At about eight weeks old I was adopted by an older couple who lived in a motor home. Even though I was their new pet, I don't think they had a clue about what a cat really needed.

There wasn't much space to roam inside my new home, and I soon learned I wasn't allowed outside. I sat in the windows to see what I was missing. Birds, mice, and other cats roamed outside, and I longed to go explore and meet them.

Then one day after my new mom and dad came back from the grocery store, they fitted me with a collar that had a stupid bell attached. I did not like this new device around my neck because it itched, and every time I moved, the bell would ring. Also, it was very hard to scratch my neck with this collar in the way.

Every time I saw something to catch and I tried to sneak up on it, my bell rang and I couldn't get close. When I tried to hide so I could sleep, this stupid bell would ring and give me away, so my owners always knew exactly where I was. As a young cat I needed a safe place to hide so I could sleep. I wasn't allowed on the bed or couch, which looked very comfortable and seemed like a good place to take a nap.

Looking out the window was my only escape.

Being confined to this motor home was stunting my growth. My new owners liked to go for daily walks, and if I got near the door when they were going outside, they always foolishly yelled at me to get away. They also yelled when I jumped up on the furniture. I soon realized that this is why I had this bell around my neck. I couldn't understand why I couldn't go with them, so I could stretch my legs and enjoy the smell of the clean fresh mountain air.

After they left, I would run up into the window to see where they were going. I have always thought it would be really cool if I could go with them, and explore the neighborhood and do my thing outdoors. I have never liked the smell of the litter they put in my litter box and I would rather go outside to do my business, so I don't have to smell the remains.

I wasn't getting the right nutrients to grow up strong and healthy because all I ever got were the leftovers of my owners' human food. I didn't realize till later in my life that there was food made specially for cats. Not getting the right nutrients when I was young made my fur dull and stunted the growth of my body and tail.

Also I never got much attention from these people except when they were yelling at me to get away from the front door. It would be nice to get a hug once in a while or get my fur brushed.

I was now ten months old and kind of lonely and undergrown for my age. Then I started thinking, "If I could get out that front door, I probably would be better off." Day or night I started looking for a chance!

Then one day when I was sitting in the window, I noticed some men working outside around my mom and dad's motor home. My owners were not paying attention when one of these men knocked and then opened the front door. I smelled the fresh mountain air and freedom lurking outside.

I finally saw my chance to bolt, so I jumped up and ran out the front door as fast as I could. Then I hid underneath the neighbor's trailer so my owners wouldn't be able to see me. My escape was flawless!

My mom heard my bell ring and yelled at me to come back, but she couldn't catch me even if she wanted to. She was too old and fat and when she looked out the front door to find me, she couldn't see me hiding. I heard the man who opened the front door apologizing to her for letting the cat out. I did not know it at the time, but apparently these men were unhooking the utilities so my mom and dad could drive away.

This was my first time outside and I couldn't wait to go explore and look for mice and birds to hunt. I was finally free of that small motorhome and the exhilaration I felt was truly awesome! Freedom never felt so good and while I was hiding waiting for it to feel safe to roam, I noticed my owners drive away in their motor home.

They were abandoning me without even taking the time to look for me. I couldn't believe how easy it was to gain my freedom and I didn't care that they were leaving me behind. I was glad to be free and after they drove away, I went out on my first walk in the clean, fresh mountain air of Buena Vista, Colorado.

I went to the bathroom for my first time outside, right under a big pine tree. What a relief! Being able to bury my stool like a good tidy cat does and then walk away from the smell was truly amazing. I couldn't wait to do it again!

So off I went to explore. I checked under all the motor homes in this RV park for mice and birds. I was excited and having a lot of fun sneaking around looking for some action. I was hungry, but every time I got near a mouse or a bird this stupid bell around my neck would ring and give me away. This made it difficult to sneak up on anything to catch.

It was starting to get dark outside after my day of hunting, so I went to find a safe place to hide and sleep. I was glad to be free even though I was extremely hungry and thirsty.

The following morning after the sun came up, I again went out exploring, looking for something tasty to eat. I went a little further this time and ended up in the forest next to the RV park. It felt safer there, and I was glad to be free so I could go check out the animals and varmints in the forest.

I hid under a big pine tree that had a unique smell, and that's when I saw my first chipmunk. I don't think it saw me hiding there and then like before, when I tried to sneak up to catch it, my bell rang and gave me away. I watched the chipmunk scurry away and climb up a pine tree close to the one I hid under. It was a fast little varmint and I think I must have scared it because it started making some strange chattering sounds.

I ran up my first tree thinking I could catch it up there. The chipmunk saw me coming and climbed up to the highest spot in this tree. I sat up there and watched it awhile before I realized that it was going to be harder getting down than it was to go up. I sharpened my claws on the tree branch that I sat on, trying to build up my courage to jump down.

After getting down, I found another pine tree to hide under that had more branches, lower to the ground. It was like a tree fort on the ground, surrounded by all these branches. I felt safe and camouflaged hiding there, so I decided to take a nap. It was a little scary out here in the big forest, but way better than being stuck inside that small motor home. After my nap, I roamed around a while to become familiar with the area. It was starting to get dark now, so I headed back to hide in the tree fort.

I realized that I was going to have to go to sleep hungry and thirsty again, but I felt it was worth being free so I could hide in the forest. During my second night outside, I was woken up by some small animals that I had never seen before. I saw a squirrel and a rabbit, and because it was so peaceful and quiet in the forest, I heard them coming well before I could actually see them. I was so excited that I started shaking.

I don't think they could see me hiding there under this tall tree, and when they came close, I could smell the differences between them. During the night I also saw several different kinds of birds that flew into the tree camouflaging me.

When I woke up the following morning, it was a bright and sunny day. I sharpened my claws on the lower branches before I took off to go exploring some more. I found a rock pile that was really fun to climb on. After sitting on top of the pile for a while, I noticed a mouse living under them. I knew I couldn't catch it with this stupid bell around my neck, so I didn't even try.

My next stop in the forest was at a log on the ground with a big hole running through it. I could smell the rabbit at the opening, and then I figured this must be where the rabbit lives. I meowed a few times, hoping it would want to come out and play. It must not have been home because it never did.

I was extremely hungry and thirsty now, and I remembered smelling another cat around this one motor home back at the RV park.

I thought maybe there would be some food around there, so I headed back to the RV park to see what I could find. I prowled around until I found the motor home with the cat smell. I looked around for a while but I couldn't find any food there, so I went up onto the front porch and started meowing.

After a couple of minutes of doing this, the woman who lived there opened the front door to see who was making all this meowing noise. She seemed really nice and kindly asked me if I was hungry. I meowed back yes, and she invited me inside to feed me some of her cat's food. This was my first time eating real cat food and I liked how it tasted. I was so hungry that I ate the entire bowl of crunchy food. I also drank up all the water in her cat's water reservoir. I didn't realize how thirsty I was until I started drinking.

When I finished feasting, I noticed her cat, Rudy, watching me from under the kitchen table. She was a beautiful orange tabby cat with a white collar. I went over to meet her and we ended up becoming friends after she showed me around the motor home. She took me to several of her hiding spots and her favorite place to sleep. Her home was bigger than the home I grew up in.

Then after a couple of hours went by, a man appeared at the front door with a strange-looking cage in his hands. I ran to hide with my new friend, but there weren't many places to do so. I was scared, and soon afterwards I was caught by this man who forced me into this cage. I guess this woman had betrayed me by calling this cat catcher and now I was being taken out to his truck.

The sound of this diesel truck really frightened me, and I wasn't sure where he was taking me. Perhaps the people who abandoned me had told this woman that I ran away, and to keep an eye out for me. I guess not, because I was taken to a place that had lots of cats in cages. I was still scared, but now I was placed into a bigger cage with food, water and a soft blanket to sleep on. This did make me feel better, and I was glad I wasn't being returned to the people who abandoned me.

I was now trapped inside a strange building surrounded by many other cats. I looked around for an escape, but that seemed impossible. I just wanted to be set free so I could head back to the forest in beautiful Buena Vista, to hunt and explore!

About thirty other cats lived around me in this building with two women who took care of us. They gave us food and water and cleaned out our cages every day.

Twice a week, several other cats and I were placed in a big room with lots of things to climb on. It had a big window with a ledge under it, and this was the highest spot in the room. The first day I was placed into this room, I immediately climbed up the carpeted log to the ledge under the window. It was nice being able to stretch out my legs and see what was going on outside.

I had to hiss and growl at this one black cat who kept trying to come up into the window with me. I did not want to share my seat or have to play with the other cats. I just wanted to be left alone so I could look out the window while I was sunning myself.

I noticed several times a day, whether or not I was in the playroom or in my cage, that people would come into the building to look at us. Once in a while, one of the cats I was living with would disappear with these strangers. I guess they were being adopted. Then I started hoping that someone would come in and like me enough to adopt me, and get me out of this cat jail.

One day, I was taken into the back room to meet the doctor. She wore a white coat with a funny long thing around her neck that she used to listen to my heartbeat. She looked into my ears, and at my teeth and also my fur coat. Then she gave me two shots in my butt, that kind of hurt! The woman who had brought me into the back room clipped a metal tag onto my collar that had some writing on it, right next to my stupid bell. Now every time I moved, I had more noise going on under my neck.

Over the next week or so, a couple more cats were brought into the building. One of these new cats was a huge black cat. He was almost twice my size and I hoped I wouldn't have to fight him for the window seat!

I was getting used to the daily routine, but I still missed being free to roam and hunt in the forest of Buena Vista. If I didn't have this bell around my neck, I think I could learn to be a sneaky, proud hunter. I felt hunting was in my blood, and I couldn't wait to catch something! The only good thing about being trapped inside this building was the food. Cat food tasted better than human food, and I noticed my fur getting softer and that I had gotten bigger since I'd been captured. One thing that I didn't like about being stuck in a cage was that after the lights went out, the nights were long and lonely. Cats were meant to prowl at night and to be stuck motionless all night was really hard on me. I truly couldn't wait to be adopted!

Chapter Two
THE GREAT ADOPTION

After several weeks had gone by that seemed like eternity, a man with a hat and sunglasses came in to view the cats. I was in the play room, sitting up in the window seat. I watched him look at and hold every cat in the caged area. I had never seen anyone be so thorough when looking at all the cats. I don't think he liked any of them, because he started to walk out of the caged area. I have a white chest, so I turned to look at him, hoping he would see me. I think he noticed me out of the corner of his eyes and that made him stop. I then saw him ask one of the ladies who took care of us, "What about these cats? Are they for adoption too?"

Then this man came into the playroom and only wanted to look at and hold me. I was very excited that he was holding me and when he looked into my eyes I could tell that this guy really liked me. I started hoping he would adopt me and make my dreams come true.

I realized while he held me, that I possessed a special gift and could look into his eyes and read his mind. He was thinking he wanted to adopt me, but couldn't do it till tomorrow. I was excited that he liked me and couldn't wait to be adopted!

After a long night of waiting, my dreams of being adopted came true. The man with the hat and sunglasses came inside and ask one of the women who took care of us if he could hold me again. While this man held me, I could read his mind, that he had owned a couple of cats before me and he was here to adopt me. I could feel he was a really cool dude and that he loved cats.

What an absolutely, unbelievable feeling it was being carried outside to this man's truck. I was so happy that he had adopted me, I sat on his lap and purred the whole ride home. This was my new dad and I could feel that he loved me because he hugged and talked to me all the way to his house. He told me that he lived up in the mountains on twenty acres of land and that he needed a good hunter to control the varmint population. I was excited to hear this, and after we got to his place, the first thing he did was take off my collar with the stupid bell. He said to me, "What kind of idiot would put a bell around a cat's neck?" I knew right then that I was going to really like this man. What a relief it was having that collar removed, and for the first time in my life, I had my neck and body brushed. Boy did that feel good!

Then to my amazement my new dad asked me if I wanted to go for a walk. I meowed back, "Yes I do!" Without yelling at me, he opened up the front door so we could go outside for a walk in the forest. He must have read my mind, because that was exactly what I was thinking. It was pure joy being free again, and truly awesome having a dad that wanted to take me with him for a walk. I ran out the front door in disbelief and I felt like the luckiest cat in the world.

I was so excited to be out in the forest again, my dad could barely keep up with me. I never knew I could run so fast, and without the bell around my neck, I couldn't wait to sneak up on something to catch. After I calmed down a bit, I found a tree to relieve myself.

That was pure heaven! I was so happy to be free again that the joy overwhelmed me. After we were out in the forest for about an hour, my dad asked me if I was hungry. I again felt like he had read my mind, because I was starving. He told me that he had a special gravy snack for me, so we headed back to the house. I have never had a gravy snack before and I couldn't wait to eat it. Then, after I wolfed it down and started cleaning my chops, I began to think, they never had anything that tasty at the cat jail!

My dad picked me up and gave me a big hug and said to me, "I am going to call you Lucky." He was thinking I was the luckiest cat west of the Mississippi River, because out of thirty cats to pick from, he chose me. I liked the name and started to purr.

When I was in cat jail, I thought after being abandoned that my purr motor was broken because every time someone held me, I just couldn't purr.

After that tasty snack, my dad showed me around the house. It was a big house with lots of room to roam. He took me into the bedroom and said that I could sleep up on his bed with the down comforter if I wanted to. I was in disbelief that he was going to allow me up there because my previous owners had always yelled at me when I did.

The next day after our morning walk in the forest, my dad told me he had to go to work and that he would be back as soon as he could. He told me that he had left me some food and water in the kitchen and to be good while he was gone.

After he left for work, I searched the entire house for a mouse to catch. I didn't find any, so I went and sat in a window to check out what was going on outside.

The view from the living room window was delightful. I could see all the way to the end of our dirt driveway. I saw several birds flying around and a chipmunk scurrying in and out collecting food down below. I watched where it went, and learned that it lived close by in a rock wall by the edge of our driveway. After sitting in the window for a while, I knew I was going to love living here.

I was feeling tired, and I remembered my dad telling me it was okay to nap on his bed. I headed into the bedroom to check out his big bed. His bed had a down comforter covering it, so I jumped up and discovered it was really fluffy and cool to the touch. I never knew duck feathers could be so comfy and warm. I stretched out as far as I could to get really comfy. It felt like I was about two feet long from paw tip to paw tip. I couldn't remember ever being this relaxed and comfortable, and I felt a real feeling of being safe for the first time in my life. I fell asleep immediately and didn't realize how tired I was, because I slept all day. Then I was woken up by my dad coming through the front door after his day at work.

I was startled when he saw me on his bed, and I wasn't sure if I should run and hide. Well, instead of being yelled at to get off his bed, he came into the bedroom and started petting me and said that I looked very comfortable and that he missed me. I was glad he wasn't angry at me for napping on his bed. He then asked me if I wanted to go outside for a walk.

I meowed back, "I sure do," and then I jumped down and stretched out. I still couldn't believe I was being allowed out the front door without anyone yelling at me. After he got something to drink, my super cool dad opened the front door so we could go for a walk.

When I got outside, I ran across the driveway to the rock wall where I had seen the chipmunk disappear earlier that day. I could smell it, and located the hole where it was hiding. This must be where it lived. I waited around for a little while to see if it would come out to play. The sun made me hot, so I ran over to the horse shed because it was in the shade. I hoped to find some mice hiding nearby. I looked and searched, but I couldn't find any. Then I ran around to the back of the horse shed, because I heard something moving back there.

Sure enough, it was a chipmunk, and I chased after it. I think I scared it because it ran really fast and hid under a big rock. This chipmunk started making some strange chattering sounds. I think it was chipmunk talk and it was saying, "You can't catch me!"

My dad was watching and then walked over to where I was, and said, "Do you want me to help you?" I meowed back, "I sure do!" He picked up a stick from under a tree and told me to get ready. I was a couple of feet away from the opening under the rock that the chipmunk vanished into. I crouched down with excitement and got myself ready to pounce. Then my dad went to the other side of the rock and stuck the stick under it to try and scare out this little varmint.

To my amazement, the chipmunk ran out from under the rock right at me. I was so excited, I quickly pounced on it and caught my very first chipmunk. I grasped it firmly in my mouth and then scurried away so I could play with it. I took it to an opening in a meadow nearby, and let it out of my mouth. I was hoping it would run so I could chase after it and catch it again. It played dead for a couple of minutes, and then like a bolt of lightning, it tried to run away. I was ready and ran as fast as I could to retrieve it.

This little varmint was fast, but I was faster. After I retrieved it, I let it go again and sure enough, it tried to run away and escape. We played together for a while and I must have caught it five or six times before it found a tree to scamper up. I ran up the tree, but I couldn't catch it.

My dad helped me catch my first chipmunk, and I was happy he did. He told me he was very proud of me for being so fast.

I soon realized I was stuck up in this tree about ten feet above the ground, because there were no branches on it to climb down. I wasn't sure how I was going to get down.

My dad was watching me the whole time, and to my amazement he walked under the tree and leaned over. He patted his back and told me to jump down onto his shoulders. He was offering me a soft platform to jump on, so I trusted him and jumped onto his back. I was so happy my new dad had helped me out of this tree, that I meowed in a way that I had never done before, thanking him for rescuing me.

He hugged me and told me he was very proud of me for being so brave and using his back to jump down out of this tall pine tree. My trust for my new dad was growing!

I then realized that I had been adopted by the coolest dad west of the Mississippi River. I felt very lucky, and my love for my new dad was becoming immeasurable. He put me down so I could prowl around some more.

I quickly noticed a blue-colored bird hiding in the long grass of the meadow that I was just playing in. I crouched down really low, and tried to sneak up to catch it. This bird must have heard me coming, because it flew away before I got close.

It was early October, and the sun was starting to go down sooner. I noticed there was a blazing red sunset and the air felt much cooler. On the way home, I heard a mouse squeak in the long grass of another meadow we were traveling through. I leaped up a couple of feet into the air to get a fix on the mouse's location. After doing that three times, I knew exactly where it was. I closed in quickly, and caught my first field mouse. It was a big one and fought me to get away, but I was hungry, so I did not let that happen. My dad commented that it was the biggest mouse he had ever seen. I played with it by tossing it up in the air and catching it several times before eating it. I always thought catching a mouse would be fun, but I never knew they were so tasty. This was my first mouse and I just couldn't wait to catch another one. I hid in the long grass, hoping I would hear another, until my dad said it was time to go home.

Hunting was easier without that stupid bell around my neck, and I was learning that I could catch just about anything that moved.

I was happy that we went for another walk in the forest so I could catch my first chipmunk and mouse. I was starting to feel like a real mountain cat, and I couldn't wait to go hunting again to improve my skills.

When we got home, my dad gave me a big bowl of crunchy giblets and another gravy snack. I think he is trying to fatten me up to help me grow up strong and healthy.

After dinner, he brushed me again, and then I sat on my dad's lap because I was starting to feel really loved. We watched a movie together before we went to sleep. When I woke up, I was thinking, I am glad I ran away from my previous owners, because my new dad knows what a cat needs. I love our daily walks together and the way he treats me.

For breakfast, my dad always ate strawberry-flavored shredded wheat cereal. I liked the way it smelled and tried to climb up to get a taste. It was all he could do to keep me away, and then after he was done eating it, he must have realized I desperately needed some extra calcium to make my bones strong. He let me drink the strawberry-flavored milk. It was so succulent tasting that I lapped it up in a fury! I did this every morning for a couple of months until my stunted tail grew out. This milk made me grow up to be big and made my fur soft and shiny.

Then one day, I just stopped drinking the strawberry-flavored milk, probably because I was getting all the right nutrients from my cat food.

I soon realized that I was a talking kitty cat with several different kinds of meows to communicate with my dad. I don't know if he was reading my mind, but he always seemed to know exactly what I was saying. I'm not sure where I learned how to talk, but I did it often. Maybe it was because my dad talked to me all the time, and I was just trying to let him know I understood him.

After breakfast, my dad opened the back door and took me out into the yard. There were three sections to the yard, surrounded by a four-foot fence. He showed me around and said he had seen a lot of mice running about back here. He told me to have fun hunting, while he went to work.

I was in disbelief that he was going to leave me in the backyard. I was very excited to be able to prowl around all day looking for mice and birds to hunt. He left me some food and water on the back porch and a comfortable down jacket to sleep on.

I felt like I was in cat heaven because I had this huge backyard to play and hunt in. After my dad was gone to work, I proceeded to explore the whole backyard. The first section I visited had a lot of pine trees. I noticed a squirrel living in one of the trees, and when I got close, the squirrel started chattering at me.

I couldn't believe how many birds flew in and out of my new hunting area. One of the other sections in my backyard had long grass and I felt totally camouflaged. I hid and snuck around, and on my first try I almost caught a bird.

Then I went to explore the other section that had two sheds. I could hear and smell mice underneath. I found a comfortable spot at the corner of one of the sheds and waited for a chance to catch another tasty mouse snack.

A few minutes went by, before I was happily surprised by a mouse. It came running out of the corner of the shed, so I quickly pounced on it. After grasping it firmly in my mouth, I headed to a grassy area by the back porch to play. I dropped it out of my mouth and proceeded to run after it. This mouse was a fast little varmint, and I enjoyed hearing it squeak every time I jumped on it.

Then, after playing with this mouse for a while, I enjoyed the second mouse snack of my life. It was as tasty as my first, and I quickly headed back to the shed for another one.

Not having that stupid bell around my neck made it very easy to sneak up on these varmints. I am becoming a very dangerous predator, and I think I have the entire mouse family living under the shed terrified that I am waiting for them.

After several tasty snacks, I was getting exhausted, so I headed to the back porch for a nap in the cool mountain air of October.

Before I fell asleep, I thought about how happy I was that my new dad trusted me enough to leave me in the backyard to hunt.

When my dad came home, he opened the back door just as I was waking up from my afternoon nap. He picked me up and gave me a big hug, and told me that he had missed me. I could read his mind that he was very happy that I was okay and still in the backyard. He asked me if I had success catching any mice, and I meowed back, "Yes I did."

Then as usual, he asked me if I wanted to go for a walk. I meowed back, "Do birds fly?" Before he put me down, I could read his mind that he never knew cats were as smart as dogs and could be walked without a leash. When he was younger, his parents had a cat and it never seemed to be very smart.

I am glad my dad takes the time to take me outside for walks so I can hunt and explore. Going out in the forest in the mountains of Colorado is a little scary, and I have to admit when we go to a new area we haven't been to before, I always let my dad lead the way just to make sure it is safe.

I love going for walks with my dad because he helps me hunt, and I feel lucky he has the patience to wait for me when I am trailing behind.

After a few weeks went by, I realized I was missing out on catching birds and other varmints by trailing behind my dad. I then started leading the way on all our walks to improve my chances at catching anything that moved.

I am becoming a sneaky, lightning-fast hunter, and every time we go out for a walk, I am catching something. One day, all in about one half hour, I caught a bird, a chipmunk, and a mouse. I think I have all the varmints around the house pretty scared.

I love living in the mountains with my dad, and I am in my glory doing what cats were born to do—hunt! My dad always tells me how proud he is of me for being such a good hunter. This makes me feel like the luckiest cat west of the Mississippi River.

I am becoming a big cat with a hunger for tasty varmints. My long legs give me an extended reach which allows me to catch just about anything that moves in my field of vision.

Then one lazy afternoon when I was napping on the bed, a friend of my dad's came over to the house. His name was Jack.

When he came into the house and walked past the bedroom doorway, my dad said, "This is my super-smart cat, Lucky," and pointed in my direction. I pretended to be asleep, so I wouldn't be disturbed by this stranger. I started listening to their conversation about me.

It was easy to hear them because they were sitting in the living room, right next to the bedroom.

I overheard my dad tell his friend that he had recently adopted me because his last cat got killed early one morning by an owl right out in the backyard, probably while he was playing with a mouse.

He also said that he thought I was the smartest and coolest cat of all the cats he had owned. He told him how good a hunter I was, and how he felt I possessed telepathy!

Then my dad told him how easily I could catch chipmunks and mice. He said I was a sneaky fast hunter, and if a chipmunk would allow me to play with it by running away and letting me catch it several times without trying to bite or fight back, that I would eventually let it run free. If it fought back or bit him, he would immediately kill it and devour it completely. Sometimes he would do the same thing with a mouse.

My dad told Jack that he thought I was a pretty smart cat to let some of these varmints go so that they would grow up to be bigger and faster. This way, he would have something to catch around the house in the future. He also told Jack that he noticed my fur got softer, shinier, and more luxurious-looking after consuming these varmints.

He told Jack several stories about how he thinks I am telepathic, and that he felt I could read his mind. One of the stories was about the time he took me to this huge rock pile near our house.

After many walks around our property, he started to trust me to stay close and listen to his commands. Then one day, he decided to take me off the property we lived on to a large rock pile. His first cats loved this, because they could be high above everything in the area and look down upon any prey available.

These rocks were about one half of a mile from the house, and they were the highest place around. He said it took his other cats several tries to figure out how to get to the top.

Then he told Jack that he thought I was telepathic, because the very first time he took me to the rock pile, he let me lead the way, and somehow I knew exactly how to get through all the boulders to the top.

There was only one way that was safe to get to the top from our side of the rock pile. This was simply amazing, and I think he must have read my mind to do that. How else would he have known how to navigate through all these big boulders to get to the top? Then, like all the other cats that I had owned, this became his favorite place to go to do some hunting.

I think Lucky feels like a mountain lion or something, because he loves to sit up there and check out the view while looking for chipmunks. The chipmunks love this area because they have a lot of places to live and hide.

Then one day, when we were hiking up through the boulders of the rock pile, we got separated after he went after a chipmunk and I couldn't keep up.

I couldn't find him after looking around for a while. I then realized I have a very special cat, because I called out his name and he amazingly talked back to me with one of his unique meows so I would know exactly where he was.

How unbelievably cool. I was surprised he was smart enough to do so. My other cats never did this, so that's when I realized he was a special, talking super cat. Even around the house, he would talk to me, and I soon learned his different meows and what they meant."

Then my dad told Jack, "There is something else that is really cool about this cat that my other cats never did. He would rather go outside to go potty than to stink up the litter box inside. This is truly saving me money, and I don't have to smell his stools or urine. What a great cat!"

I ended up falling back asleep after I found out my dad thought I was such an awesome cat.

* * *

After I woke up from my nap, I started thinking about how close my new dad and I were getting. He trusted me to stay close to him on our walks in the forest. I truly love it when he takes me to the huge rock pile. It is building up my muscle strength and I am learning that I can jump up four to five feet onto a boulder. I think that the chipmunks who live in and around these large boulders are going to have to start worrying about me catching them.

Because I am such a good cat who has a lot of energy, my dad has started to take me on longer walks, over a mile through the forest to various rock formations. I am having fun, and these long walks are making me as hungry as a horse! I truly feel like a lean, clean hunting machine!

One day, when I was out hunting on one of our long walks through the forest, we encountered a herd of mule deer. I had never seen a mule deer before, and I thought I could sneak up on them. I did not think they saw me when I tried to creep up behind them, but I soon realized that they knew I was there and were watching me very closely. They must have been intimidated by my sneakiness, because a few of them started to run away. Then to my amazement, the dominant ones in the herd ganged up on me and started running after me. I guess they were frightened by me stalking them, and it became obvious that they wanted to hurt me because they were trying to hoof me to death. I had to zig and zag and then quickly run up the nearest tree to avoid being trampled.

Then I realized my dad had my back, because he quickly stepped in and started chasing them away. I never knew my dad could run so fast. He ran after them, yelling at them until they disappeared into the forest.

He came over to the tree I was hiding in to rescue me. I jumped down onto his back and he asked me if I was all right. He said, "You learned a valuable lesson today. Never hunt something that is bigger than you."

Then we walked to a rock formation that we had never been to before that had a whole family of chipmunks living there. I tried to catch a couple of these varmints, but they were really fast and had too many hiding spots.

On the way home, we passed by our neighbor's house that is usually vacant. I ran over to the front porch to see if any varmints were hiding under it. As soon as I got near the porch, a chipmunk went running along the railing and up a tree. My dad followed me over there to see if he could help. I squeezed under the front porch to see if anything was hiding under there. As soon as I did, a big rabbit bolted out from underneath and ran to a nearby shed.

I haven't seen any rabbits since I moved into my new home, so I started sniffing around the shed to remember what these varmints smelled like. Rabbits have a unique smell, and I cannot wait to catch one. I prowled around for a while and knew this was going to be a great hunting spot because I could smell rabbits, mice, and chipmunks everywhere!

My dad called for me to come, and then we headed back to the house for a snack. I love these tasty gravy snacks because they are making my fur soft and shiny. After dinner, my dad brushed me and then let me out into the backyard so I could do some more hunting.

I love living in the mountains of Colorado and all the luxuries I am now enjoying. All my memories of motor home living are quickly vanishing. To live in a big house with room to roam is truly awesome.

My dad likes to leave the bedroom window partially open, which makes it cool in there to sleep. It was now the third week in October, and the cool mountain air was refreshing. At night, I have been sleeping next to my dad on top of the fluffy down comforter. It is awesome that he lets me do this, because he is very warm and I am sleeping better than I ever have.

In the cool night time air, I have been working on growing out my winter coat. My summer coat is thinner and my fur has lots of white hairs mixed in with my gray and black ones. The white hairs help reflect the sunlight which makes me cooler. My winter coat is thicker, and instead of having white hairs mixed in, I replaced them with black ones. This helps absorb the sunlight which makes me warmer. How smart is that!

Today is October 28th, and in the morning my dad tells me he thinks I am about a year old and because it is his birthday today, it will also be mine. How awesome is that, to celebrate our birthdays together on the same day!

Then my dad gave me a big birthday hug and told me he has bought me a new kind of gravy. It was in a can instead of a squeeze package. He opened it up and said he would give me half for breakfast and the other half for dinner. It was very tender tuna in a special gravy sauce. My birthday present was incredibly scrumptious, and I quickly wolfed it down. I was so happy and satisfied that I couldn't wait until dinner time.

After our morning walk in the cool crisp October air, I felt completely filled with joy. My dad had to go to work, so I decided to go take a nap on that soft, fluffy down comforter. During my nap, I dreamed about catching a stinky, long-eared rabbit and the succulent taste of my birthday gravy snack.

When my dad came home from work, he gave me the rest of my tuna gravy snack. It was as delicious and tasty as it was this morning. I am hoping he will buy this new kind of gravy again.

The next day, my dad told me he had to work on his truck out in the garage. He said that if I stayed around, he would let me explore by myself out in the front yard. I was excited he trusted me enough to let me roam around while he worked.

It was unbelievably nice outside today because the sun has warmed the temperature up into the sixties. After my dad opened the large garage door to let the light in, I immediately headed towards the horse shed to see what I could find. When I got near the shed, I smelled a rabbit so I crouched down and slowly prowled towards an opening under the shed.

Then, like a bolt of lightning, this big rabbit darted out from beneath the horse shed. I tried to pounce on it, but I just missed. I watched where it went, and followed it to a big log on the ground that had a hole running through it. The rabbit ran inside the log and disappeared. I slowly and quietly prowled to the end of the log. I looked inside and realized the opening was big enough for me to fit. I could really smell this rabbit, so I headed inside to see if I could find it. When I got about halfway through the log, I could hear the rabbit exiting out the other side. I hurried through, but when I got outside, the rabbit had vanished into the forest.

I prowled around looking for other varmints to catch. I noticed a big black squirrel running from one pine tree to another. I headed towards these trees to find out what the squirrel was doing. When I sat below this one pine tree, the squirrel started chattering and looking at me.

The only other squirrel that I have ever seen is a small brown squirrel when I was hiding in the forest of Buena Vista. This black squirrel was a lot bigger, and then it did something that intrigued me. This squirrel knew I was watching, and it slowly started sneaking down the other side of the tree, periodically looking around to see if I was still sitting there. I was intensely watching as it got close to me.

When it came down to about four feet above me, I was thinking I could just about jump up this tree and grab it. For some reason, it kept coming around the tree, chattering and looking at me. It did this several times, while flipping its tail up and down, trying to antagonize me into attacking. It quickly became obvious to me that this squirrel wasn't afraid, and wanted me to play.

Every time I ran up the tree to catch it, the squirrel ran up higher and started chattering even louder, trying to say, "You can't catch me." After a couple of attempts to catch it, I gave up my efforts. This squirrel was a bully, and truly wasn't afraid of me.

Then I heard my dad calling for me. The first time he called I hesitated, because I was having so much fun. But being free to roam and prowl was truly a privilege that I didn't want to ruin, so the second time he called for me I headed to the front door. When I arrived, he praised me for coming when he called.

He picked me up and gave me a big hug, and said, "You're a smart cat for coming so soon." He also told me that he loves me and that he thinks I am getting bigger.

When we got inside, he brushed me again. I really like getting brushed, because it feels good and it is making my fur coat very soft and shiny.

Later that evening, after it was dark and the full moon was up, my dad asked me if I wanted to go for a moonlit walk. I meowed back, "Yes I do," so he put his coat on and out we went into the cool evening air. We usually never went out front into the forest at night because of all the danger present. There are mountain lions, foxes, coyotes and big owls that are very hungry this time of the year. With winter setting in, the hunting for these creatures is getting scarce.

My dad told me to stay close as we headed up our long driveway to the main dirt road that we lived on. When we got on the road, I was having a blast walking in the moonlight while searching for something to catch. My dad said that I was easier to see in the moonlight than his other cats. Both his other cats were dark, tiger-striped without any white on them. Because I have white paws, he said that when I was trotting along my legs looked like a flurry of moving polka dots. Even at a distance, he said he could see me moving in the moonlight and that it looked really cool.

We ended up walking all the way down to the end of our dirt road. On the way back, my dad allowed me to go onto our neighbor's property for a short visit.

She has five cats, and four of them are female. I have always wanted to sneak around her house to get a smell of her cats' scent. The only time her cats get to go outside was during the day, because she worked nights. They were confined to a caged area and were not as lucky as I, being allowed to go out for walks.

She was afraid for them, because she had already lost several cats to a mountain lion that sometimes lived in and around the huge boulder pile my dad took me to. One time, when we were exploring around these huge boulders, we came across one of her dead cat's remains. The only things left to this cat were its teeth and part of its tail.

After a short visit sneaking around her cats' caged area in the moonlight, my dad called for me to come. I knew I should leave immediately, because my dad usually never let me go onto her property to explore, because he couldn't come with me to watch my back. He didn't want to be seen trespassing on our neighbor's property, so I headed out to the dirt road where my dad was waiting for me. He was very proud of me for coming when he called.

I was definitely hoping he would let me do that again, because I enjoyed smelling the other cats my neighbor owned. Going for a walk in the moonlight was a real blast, and even though I didn't catch anything, I have to admit I truly enjoyed the experience.

After watching a movie, my dad went into the bedroom to go to sleep. I always follow him in, because I like to sleep next to him on top of the down comforter. He is nice and warm, and I enjoy snuggling up next to him in the cool October air that comes through the bedroom window.

This window is always cracked open to let in the fresh mountain air. Even though the air is cold, I like having the window slightly open, because with my keen hearing I can hear what is going on outside. This window has a ledge under it, and with the window blind up about a foot, it is easy to jump up onto it in the middle of the night to see what is going on outside.

One night I was woken up by some noise outside, and when I jumped onto the window ledge, I saw a fox sniffing around the front yard. It was probably looking for me. I was glad I was inside where it was safe. On another night when I was looking out the window, I saw a rabbit by our woodpile. It hopped over near the front porch, right under my window. I felt excited, and wished the window was open far enough so I could jump out and catch it. Then I heard it hop underneath the front porch, and start digging in the dirt.

In the morning when we went out for a walk, I immediately ran under the porch to see if Mr. Rabbit was hiding under there. I could smell it, but it wasn't there.

The next night when I was comfortably asleep next to my dad, I was woken up by the wind howling. I did not know it then, but in the morning I realized that the wind had blown in a snowstorm. When we went out for a walk, there was an inch of fresh snow on the ground. This was my first time seeing snow, and I wasn't sure what to think of this cold stuff.

I ventured out into this sea of cold white and soon realized that it was making my paws numb. I also noticed that wherever I went, I left paw prints behind me, making fresh tracks in the snow. My dad said I looked like a powder hound, because I was having so much fun running through the freshly fallen snow.

When we got home from our morning walk, my dad started a fire in the wood-burning stove. It was the first fire of the year, and it felt good to lay in front of it and warm up my cold paws. This was the first time in my life that I have gotten to enjoy the heat that comes off from a wood stove, and it felt awesome after our cool morning walk in the snow.

The door of this wood stove has a glass face, and it was really intense watching the wood burn behind it. Seeing the fire inside was frightening, but the joy of the heat I felt was worth it.

After getting warmed up in front of the fire, my dad asked me if I wanted to take a bath. I wasn't sure what that meant, so I read his mind. He was thinking I needed a bath because I probably have never had one, and with the wood burning stove going, that would dry me off quickly.

He was right. I have never been given a bath before, so I thought, why not? I did feel a little bit dirty. After I got over the shock of being placed in warm, soapy water, I have to admit I started to enjoy it. Being completely wet, rubbed down, and washed was a new experience for me that I think I can tolerate again. After my bath, I was partially dried off with a towel and then my dad placed me in front of the warm wood stove so I could finish drying. The heat felt good and I dried off amazingly quick.

Then he brushed me several times to get the knots out of my fur. I felt incredibly clean, and my fur looked luxuriously soft and shiny.

My dad said that he thinks that I am a crazy cat because I seemed to like being given a bath! His other cats hated bathing, and would fight and claw him whenever he tried.

I was so happy after taking a bath that I jumped onto my dad's lap and started rubbing my head against his chest in appreciation for what he had just done. I laid down and purred furiously until I fell asleep. What a super cool dad I have. I sure love the way he takes care of me.

When I woke up, I felt like a million bucks having been freshly bathed. Now I truly am a lean, clean, hunting machine!

I am a fifteen-pound super cat who eats like a horse. With all the crunchy cat food, gravy snacks and varmints I eat, one would think that I would be a lazy fat cat. My dad said I eat as much as the big dog he used to have.

I say, "I am still a growing boy and with all the energy, exercise and hunting I do, who wouldn't be as hungry as I am?" I seem to be inexhaustible in my attempts to hunt down and catch the varmints who lived around here. I truly feel lucky to be alive and I love the opportunity I get to go hunting every day with my dad.

Being born and raised in the mountains of Colorado is simply exhilarating. I can't imagine being stuck in an apartment or a city and not having anywhere to hunt or roam.

Not having the freedom to be stimulated by the great outdoors, I think would be excruciating and I feel bad for all the cats who are stuck inside all their lives.

Today is Saturday, and on our morning walk through the forest, we stopped by the neighbor's house that is usually vacant. We have been to this house several times over the last couple of weeks mainly because I lead the way and my dad follows. I like exploring around this house because of all the varmints I have caught. With nobody living there on a regular basis, the varmints have moved in and made it their home. I can always smell the scent of the rabbit every time I am there, and I am bound and determined to catch one of these long-eared, stinky varmints.

I have caught and eaten many mice, several chipmunks, and a rat, but never the rabbit or the squirrel. It is hard to get close to a squirrel, with them living so high up in the pine trees. I have noticed when they are down on the ground, that they are very fast and don't stay long. On several occasions, I have almost caught the mighty rabbit. I think my chances of doing so would improve greatly if I had more time to wait for one outside their rabbit hole.

The snow we got the other day melted away quickly, so when we got home from our walk my dad put me out into the backyard. I have seen several rabbits out there, but every time I have tried to catch one, they scurried away under the fence or the sheds to avoid being caught. Today when I was sneaking around, I saw a baby rabbit hiding outside my backyard fence. This fence that contained me to my yard was four feet high, and because I am so strong, I thought that I could probably jump right over and catch this little rabbit.

On my first try, I jumped over like it wasn't even there. The rabbit saw me, and bolted into a small hole under a big rock. I sniffed around for a while, and then I tried to reach into the hole with my long paw to try and snag the baby rabbit. I was unsuccessful, so I decided to prowl over to the neighbor's vacant house to see if I could catch one of the rabbits that lived over there.

Without the noise that my dad makes when he walks with his big boots, and having more time to hunt, I think I might get lucky and catch one. These rabbits have eluded me so far, but today I am hoping I will have more success. As soon as I got over there, I located the fresh smell of a rabbit and decided to hide by a low-lying branch next to its hole going into the ground. I felt camouflaged by the branch, so I sat, looked and listened for one to come out and play.

I waited patiently by this hole and was there for a while, but I didn't see any stinky, long-eared rabbits.

Then, to my amazement here comes my dad walking briskly towards me. I wasn't sure if he had seen me yet, so I crouched down in an attempt to hide. When he got to the neighbor's house, he called for me, but I didn't come because I wasn't sure if I was in trouble for jumping over the fence. He looked around for a while, and eventually saw me hiding by the tree branch. Then my dad quickly came over to where I was and picked me up. He told me that he thought I might be over here because I wasn't in the backyard. He said he was glad I was all right, and then started carrying me towards our house. On the way home, he told me how dangerous it was for me to be out roaming around on my own and how he had lost his other cats to the hungry wildlife that lived around here. He also said that I wouldn't have a chance to survive if a predator saw me out there by myself without your dad being close by to protect you.

I could tell he was upset with me for jumping over the fence, because he carried me all the way home.

After looking into his eyes, I could read his mind, and I knew that my dad was telling me the truth about the danger from all the predators that hunted in the forest. I understood what he was saying to me, and being the intelligent cat that I am, I decided to never jump over the fence again.

Over the next week or so, I noticed that my dad kept a watchful eye on me whenever I was allowed in the backyard. I guess he wanted to make sure I wasn't going to jump over the fence again.

Then after a while, I think he felt he could trust me again, because he stopped watching me so closely. Maybe he read my mind and realized that I wasn't planning on jumping over any more fences.

With winter coming, I have seen more rabbits hopping around in my backyard than I ever have. Over the last couple of weeks, I have noticed several new holes dug under the sheds and fence, and I can smell the scent of the rabbit near them. I've been hoping to catch this elusive varmint for a long time, and it is weird that they are now coming into my back yard after the fence jumping incident! I have been spending more time in my back yard, vigorously prowling around and waiting for a chance to catch one. I am so excited, that I can hardly sleep at night and I've been staying outside longer after dark than usual to increase my chances of surprising one of these stinky, long-eared rabbits.

Then one sunny day, when I was laying in the grass sunning myself, I heard a noise over by the sheds. I jumped up and quietly prowled over to them, and that's when I smelled the scent of a rabbit near the opening under one of the sheds. I was very excited, and when I got close to the opening, the baby rabbit that I had seen outside the fence a few weeks ago bolted out. I pounced on it so hard that the impact of me doing so killed it. I guess I don't know my own strength, because I really wanted to play with it before I found out if rabbits were tasty.

I was so happy that I finally caught my first rabbit, that instead of eating it, I took it to the back porch to show my dad. I meowed a few times to get his attention, and after a while he came out the back door to see what all the noise was about.

When he saw the rabbit laying there at his feet, he started rubbing my neck and praising me for being such a fast and sneaky cat. I felt exhilarated and couldn't wait to do it again! Then he said that he was very proud of me for catching it, because the rabbits were digging holes under the fence and sheds. He also said he was proud of me for staying in the back yard.

I was so excited about catching this rabbit, that I went back to the sheds for the rest of the day to see if there were any more hiding there.

In the evening when it started to get dark, my dad called for me to come, because he had a special snack for me. I was starving after my long day of hunting, so I ran inside to wolf down a tasty gravy snack. It was that special gravy out of a can, and he said that this was for me catching the rabbit. He thanked me for doing so and said that he hoped I would catch any other rabbits trying to dig holes under the fence or the sheds. What a cool dad who would thank me for doing what I love to do!

Then over the next few days when I was out in the back yard, I could hear my dad working on something in the garage. On the third day, he opened up the gate to the backyard and carried out this big box-looking thing. I was thinking, what the heck was this strange looking box? He had built me a two-story cat fort with windows.

He placed it between two pine trees about eight feet above the ground.

He secured the cat fort to the trees by nailing in two rails beneath, and then nailing the fort to the rails. I watched him do this while he was standing eight feet above the ground in the trees, next to my cat fort. He nailed in two shelves at different heights, one on one tree, and one slightly higher on the other.

He took me over to the cat fort and said that he has made this for me. He told me that all I have to do to get into it was jump up onto the first shelf and then up to the other one that is across and slightly higher. These shelves have carpet stapled to them for traction.

I was now very curious as to what this box-looking thing with windows was! When my dad headed back to the garage, you could say "curiosity got the cat"! I am a great tree climber and I needed to know what was up in this new cat fort. I jumped up three feet onto the first shelf on one tree, and then up and across another three feet to the second shelf on the other tree. Now I was right below this cat fort and I only had another two feet left to jump up into the bottom floor. About one third of the bottom floor was open, so it was like a third shelf. I leaped into the cat fort, and that's when I discovered the bottom floor was carpeted and had little windows on either side.

How cool is that! The bottom floor is a big room, one-and-a-half feet wide by two feet long with plexi-glass covering the windows.

There is an angled ramp towards the back of the bottom floor that allows me to get to the top floor. I climbed up the ramp into the upper floor. This floor was spacious, and was one-and-a-half feet wide by two-and-a-half feet long. It had a really comfy blanket secured to the floor, and a big viewing window that also had a plexi-glass covering.

I was very excited, and I liked what I saw. I laid down on the soft comfy blanket and gazed out the big viewing window.

I couldn't believe the great view and how comfy and cool my new fort was.

My dad must really love me to spend the time to make me such an awesome, safe cat fort. Now I have a place of my own to hide and sleep when I am out in the back yard.

Then I saw my dad walking towards me through the window. When he got below the fort, he said to me that he could see me up there, and wasn't surprised that I was already checking it out.

I meowed back several times, thanking him for this stylish cat fort. I felt so comfy and safe, that I ended up taking a nap. When I woke up and started to head down, I noticed that my dad had put a small bowl of water and food on the bottom floor for me.

What a great dad!

I feel like the luckiest cat west of the Mississippi River and I am truly in cat heaven. After jumping down, I went to find my dad to give him some of my love and appreciation.

The next day, I sat by the back door because I wanted my dad to let me out back so I could climb up and enjoy my new cat fort. This time when I climbed back up into my fort, I decided to check out the bottom floor. I liked the two windows on this floor because I could see towards the house like on the top floor and out the other window, I could see all the way to the back of my yard, where all the pine trees were located.

This floor was carpeted, so when I lay down it is very comfy. The view was great, and I could see down below my fort through the opening in the bottom floor.

I was in the top spot, and now if anything moved anywhere in my back yard, I would be able to see them. How cool is that? My dad was really thinking when he designed this cat fort for me. Meow-who!

Chapter Three
THE LONG WINTER

It is now mid-November, and I love living in the mountains of Colorado. With the shorter days and the cooler air temperature, I can feel that winter is close.

Thanks to my dad, my winter coat is almost complete. He brushes me often which has helped me shed out my summer coat. Those tasty gravy snacks that he feeds me are making my fur soft and shiny. Leaving the bedroom window cracked open at night, and those cold morning walks have also helped my fur grow in thick.

According to my dad, when you live at 9,300 feet above sea level you have to be prepared for big winter storms, deep snow, and colder temperatures. Winter up here has a tendency to catch you off guard. On any given day it can be sunny and nice outside, then within a couple of hours it could change to cold and snowy.

Because of the colder temperatures, my morning and evening walks have been shortened. I have not seen as many varmints to catch than I did in the summer months. I guess they don't like the cold and only come out around midday, if the sun is out. I think that is why I don't see them as often, because I am usually napping at this time.

I have also noticed that the time I spend in the backyard has been shortened, and I don't see as many mice as I did in the summertime. I must have eaten most of them, or maybe I have them all so frightened that they don't come out as often.

When I am out in the backyard, I have been spending most of my time on the second floor of my cat fort. The big window up there faces south and lets the sun in most of the day. I enjoy napping in the sunlight, because it keeps me warm and toasty.

I have noticed the squirrels who lived in the pine trees have been coming into my fort when I am not home. I can smell them, and they have been eating my food and drinking my water. I hope that they will come in and do this when I am home! I would love to catch one of those super-fast varmints stealing my food.

Today is Saturday, and I am hanging out with my dad. He invited me to come out into the garage with him because he said he has seen some mice out there, and he wants me to catch them. He told me that because it has been so cold outside, the mice have been sneaking into the garage to stay warm.

I was very excited to hear this, so I started searching around. I could smell mice around the storage boxes and paint cans, and after prowling around a while I finally scared one out. I couldn't catch it because it ran up the wall towards the attic.

My dad saw this mouse scurry away and told me that he would make it possible for me to get up into the attic. I thought, "Really? How can you do that?"

I read his mind and he was thinking, "Watch and you will see!" He pulled out an old mattress and turned it upright so the long part of the mattress stood up. He secured it to the wall by the corner of the garage. Then he got on a ladder and nailed in a wooden shelf in between the vertical 2x4 studs just above the mattress.

Now there was a shelf I could jump up onto halfway between the top of the mattress and the attic.

I was so excited about what my dad had just done for me, that I quickly ran up to the top of the soft mattress using my claws.

Then I jumped up two feet onto the shelf, and then another two feet up onto the rafters inside the attic.

I was now sitting in the attic on some wide boards that went across the top of the rafters. I had a great view of the entire garage, and could look down upon my super-cool dad.

He said that I was very smart for figuring out how to get up there so quickly! Now the mice had nowhere to hide.

The wide boards going across the top of the rafters made it easy to roam about up there. Then, being the qualified hunter that I am, I soon located the mouse in the corner of the attic. It quivered in disbelief that I was up there, staring it down.

This was a big tasty-looking mouse that didn't have many options to escape. I walked on a wide board going across the rafters, and using my cunningness, I tricked the mouse into thinking I was going left, forcing it to go right. I then nabbed it with my extended reach, and after getting it firmly in my grasp, I headed down to the top of the mattress for a well-deserved tasty mouse snack.

I was starving for a mouse, and after devouring it, I noticed my dad seemed very excited that his work to get me up in the attic had paid off. He came over to where I was resting on top of the mattress and reached up and patted me on my head, thanking me for a job well done.

I meowed back, thanking him for helping me catch this elusive mouse. What a cool dad I have.

Now, whether or not it is snowing or cold outside, I have a place for hunting mice in the winter time. I was very excited about my new hunting spot and I couldn't wait to help out my dad by catching another one.

Being up on top of the mattress gave me a good view of the entire garage. I sat up there and looked and listened while my dad finished some work that he was doing on his truck.

It was so soft and comfy up on top of this mattress, that I decided to stretch out and take a nap. I dreamed that there was an entire mouse family living in the garage, and how I eventually caught them all.

The next day on our morning walk, it was quite chilly outside. To warm us up, I decided to take my dad on a lengthy walk to the boulder pile.

A ridge of rocks runs south of the boulder pile, and is slightly lower in height. Instead of heading up to the top of the boulder pile, I led my dad south down the ridge. I decided to go this way because I have more success catching chipmunks on the ridge than the boulder pile.

About halfway down this ridge I spotted my first chipmunk sunning itself on a rock. I crouched down and quietly approached the rock, hoping to catch it off guard. I think it must have heard my dad walking towards us with his big winter boots, because it quickly bolted under the rock. My dad's boots do make a lot of noise when he is walking through the forest and most of the time, I can tell exactly where he is just by this sound without looking.

I think my dad realized his boot noise scared away the chipmunk I was hunting, because he quickly offered to help me catch it. He asked me if I was ready, then he leaned down on the other side of the rock and started blowing loudly into the hole underneath. About a month ago, my dad started blowing loudly into the chipmunks' holes because it seemed to frighten them more than a stick does.

I crouched down quickly, and sure enough, after my dad blew into the hole the chipmunk came running out towards me. I immediately pounced on it and caught this chipmunk for breakfast. I usually like to play with them before I eat them, but because I hadn't caught one in a while, I decided to devour it quickly. Chipmunks are very tasty to eat, and this one filled my stomach right up!

My dad was sitting nearby on a flat rock trying to stay warm in the sun. The ridge we were on is longer than it was wide. In some spots, you could see to the bottom of the valleys on both sides.

This ridge was a hundred yards high, which made the views awesome and the hunting great.

It was bitter cold outside, even though the sun shone brightly. After I finished my morning snack, I jumped onto my dad's lap to stay warm and thank him for helping me.

While I was warming up my paws on my dad's lap, I thought about how the two of us make an awesome hunting team! I purred furiously, trying to thank him. My feelings of love and appreciation were truly immeasurable.

Then, while I sat in my dad's lap purring, he did something I wasn't expecting. He asked me if I was cold, and then opened his coat to try and cover me. The zipper on his coat is broken, so he uses the snap buttons instead.

Because the wind was blowing so strong and cold, I decided to climb inside his coat to stay warm. The bottom snap of his coat was secured, and when I looked inside it seemed like a cat fort. I went in head first as far as I could go, and then turned around so that my head faced out while my body snuggled right next to his. He was very warm and I felt safe and protected from the cold. I was now completely inside his coat on his left side with just my nose sticking out. I liked what I had accomplished because I felt toasty warm and I still had a good view of my surroundings.

My dad was happily surprised that I was smart enough to pull off this maneuver, because I was a big cat and I barely had the room to do this. My dad hugged me and said, "You are a super smart cat for figuring out how to get inside my coat to stay toasty warm."

With the bottom button of his coat snapped closed, I felt very warm and safe because it held me so I couldn't fall out. I was in cat heaven because with a full belly I was completely comfy and warm inside my dad's coat with an awesome view of the ridge and valley below.

Throughout the cold winter months, I continued to pull off this coat maneuver any time I saw the chance. Having a place to warm myself up on our daily walks in the cold is truly awesome and

I feel like the luckiest cat west of the Mississippi River. I love my dad for being so warm and thoughtful.

I also have another maneuver that I use when there is snow on the ground or my paws get cold. I will climb a tree and pretend to be stuck. Sometimes I have to meow to get my dad's attention, but most of the time he knows where I am and comes to rescue me. He always comes over to the tree that I am in and lets me jump down onto his back. Sometimes the jump can be as much as four to five feet in distance. Then I will sit on his back for a few minutes to warm up my cold paws. When the jump down is a big one, my dad always comments to me that I am a brave cat.

I think he can read my mind, because he seems to know what I am doing. He will stay leaned over instead of standing back up like he does in the summertime. This gives me a soft, warm and comfy place to warm myself up.

What a super cool dad for realizing this and allowing me to rest on his back for several minutes to keep warm.

When we got home from our walk to the rock ridge, my dad made us a fire in the wood stove. After being outside in the cold it felt wonderful to sit by the fire and get warmed.

The next day when I woke up, I could tell it was another cold day outside. The air coming through the slightly opened bedroom window was frigid, and made me feel like staying next to my warm dad instead of getting up for breakfast.

After we got up, we sat by the toasty warm wood stove and enjoyed our breakfast.

Today on our morning walk through the woods, I decided to head out behind our house to a grassy ridge. It is warmer on this ridge because the sun hits there first thing in the morning. Without any trees blocking the sunlight, it was easy to stay warm prowling down the east side of this ridge.

When we got down to a rock outcropping, my dad noticed the hair on my back and neck was standing up, and that I was acting kind of strangely!

I stopped prowling when I smelled fear, and after sniffing the air intensely, I felt scared. I smelled blood!

I felt fear, so I took off running towards the house. My dad couldn't keep up, and several minutes later he arrived back at the house where I was waiting for him on the front porch.

He told me he understood why I took off running so quickly. He said that after I left, he stood on top of the rock outcropping and could see down below the remains of a big mule deer. Apparently, a mountain lion had hunted it down and killed it during the previous night. The kill spot was fresh because the blood was still red and not yet dried. Blood was spattered everywhere, and body parts strewn all over the place.

I knew I smelled blood, and after we went inside to get warm I could sense my dad was worried. He was worried about our safety because the mountain lion might still be in the area waiting for a chance to come back and finish what it hadn't eaten.

Over the next few days, I noticed that my dad brought his gun with him on our daily walks.

I was very curious about what had happened to this mule deer. Was this one of the five deer that grazed around the property? After a week or so went by, I built up the nerve to head back down to the kill spot and check it out.

All that was left of this mule deer was its head, rib cage and legs. I was very scared and couldn't believe what my eyes were seeing! I was still frightened by the smell, so I decided to leave immediately, looking over my shoulder as I left.

Now that I have seen the evidence that there are hungry mountain lions roaming and hunting in this area near our house, I've been more cautious and alert on our daily walks or when I am hunting.

The following day on our evening walk, I saw the herd of mule deer that usually hangs out around our property. The herd of five mule deer that I frequently saw grazing on our daily walks was now down to four. Two adult females and two adolescent mule deer were left. One of the younger deer was albino, and must have felt safe from predators when there was snow on the ground. The white in its fur made it stand out like a sore thumb when the ground was bare. I have seen it several times grazing around the property and I always see this one first while the others are camouflaged with their brown bodies on a brownish background. On the other hand, in the winter time when there is snow on the ground, this albino deer is almost invisible while the others aren't.

It is a cool-looking deer, and I have to wonder if its fur will stay white all its life.

Something else that I think is cool, is that sometimes when we are out on our walks, I have noticed a lone mule deer who follows us around. It is odd seeing just one deer in the forest, and I think this deer must feel safe traveling around with us. The first time I saw the deer following us, I was a little scared, but after a while I realized that it was just curious as to what we were doing out here in the forest.

Because this deer follows us around so often, I am starting to think that it likes hanging out with us. Maybe it thinks we will adopt it and make it part of our herd. What a crazy deer!

My dad has also noticed this deer following us, and thinks that this is strange behavior for any deer. It isn't like we have any food or anything.

Today on our way home from our morning walk, I saw that big rabbit again. Instead of being by the horse shed, it was sitting down by the culvert that went under our dirt driveway. The culvert was one foot in diameter and about twelve feet long. I have smelled this rabbit down there on several occasions, and I have walked through the pipe many times looking for it.

My dad is entertained when he has seen me going through the culvert, and calls it the cat tunnel.

I sneakily headed down the driveway to where I saw the rabbit. When I got close, it saw me and bolted up the hillside and disappeared.

I hope someday I will catch this big rabbit.

After we got home and went inside, I decided to take a nap on the couch in front of the wood burning stove. I have seen my dad lying on the couch with his back towards the heat of the wood stove, so today I thought I would try this out myself.

I stretched out with my back facing the toasty warm wood stove, and then I placed my paws against the back of the couch to push myself towards the heat. I can see why my dad does this, because the intense heat feels really good on my back after our cold morning walk through the forest.

After my dad made a phone call to one of his friends, he saw me sprawled out on the couch in front of the wood stove getting nice and warm. He grabbed the brush and started brushing my warm back. Then he said, "You're in my spot, and it looks like you are imitating me, you copycat!" I felt delighted he noticed.

He will probably have to fight me for this spot in the future, because this is definitely comfortable.

I am truly glad my dad adopted me because I love the way he takes care of me.

Today when my dad opened the front door for our morning walk, there was a large animal standing across the driveway near the horse shed. Instead of running out the front door like I usually do, I stopped about halfway out to see what this big creature was doing.

Then when I was sitting on the front porch, my dad commented, "Do you see that horse over there?" I meowed back, "I sure do." I was wondering what this large animal was, and now that I knew it was a horse, I was thinking, what is it doing in our front yard?

My dad wasn't afraid of this large animal and walked across the driveway to meet it. When he got near it, he started talking to it and then started rubbing its neck. Then he said to me, "I think this horse is thirsty." He went up to the garage and got a five-gallon bucket. After filling it with water, he placed it in front of the horse. Sure enough, it was thirsty, because it drank the whole bucket in just a couple of minutes. After drinking the water, this horse must have been hungry too, because it started chewing on some of the long grass near the horse shed.

After we came back from our morning walk, this horse was still hanging out by the shed. I was a little frightened that this large creature was still in our front yard and I started thinking, I wonder where this horse came from, because I have never seen it before today.

Then my dad said, "It looks like this horse either used to live here or was boarded here, because it seems right at home." This couldn't be a coincidence, because how else would it know how to get up here and then to hang out by the shed that had horse stalls inside?

The horse hung out with us for a couple of days and then vanished without a trace. After eating all the grass around the shed, I think it must have gotten hungry and headed back to where it lived. At least now I know what a horse looks and smells like.

It is now early December, and the weather has become extremely nice. It has been sunny and in the mid-sixties. I have been hanging out in the backyard doing what I love to do—hunt for varmints.

Then on one of these sunny afternoons when I was relaxing up in my cat fort, I saw something move over by one of the sheds through the opening in the bottom floor of my cat fort.

I jumped down to go investigate, and when I reached the shed I saw what looked like a rabbit with a big fluffy white tail. I was excited and quietly approached this funny-looking rabbit. Then, just before it disappeared under the shed, it lifted its tail and sprayed out a horridly stinky smell. Some of this stinky mist got into my eyes and on my face. It stung horribly and made my eyes water. I tried cleaning my eyes with my paws, and then I tried rolling in the grass to rid myself of the awful smell. Nothing I did seemed to work, and that nasty smell remained.

When my dad got home from work, he immediately smelled the stench on me. Then he said, "You must have been chasing after a skunk. Never chase a varmint that has a stripe down its back and tail. Hopefully, you have learned your lesson and won't do that again."

After starting a fire in the wood stove, my dad gave me a long bath. During the bath, he said that I was lucky I didn't get hit head on by this skunk's spray, because the smell would have been a lot worse. He told me a story about his dog getting sprayed by a skunk, and even after three baths he still had that horrible smell on him. It took months before the dog's smell disappeared. Thankfully after my bath, I only had a slight odor of skunk left on me.

My dad went out into the back yard to see how the skunk had managed to get into the yard. He saw that it had dug a hole under the fence and was probably going to use the shed as a winter hideout.

Then to his amazement, when he went over by the sheds, he saw the skunk. It was stuck between the shed and some chicken wire that surrounded the bottom of one of these sheds. He said to the skunk, "What are you doing in my back yard?" From about three feet away from the skunk, he pulled up the chicken wire from the ground in hopes the skunk would eventually get free and go find another spot in the forest to camp out for the winter.

When he came back inside, my dad said that I must have really scared the skunk, because after going under the shed, it tried to escape out the back side and got caught in between the shed and the chicken wire.

He also said that he had never seen a skunk that looked like this one. Instead of being black with a white stripe, it was white with brown polka dots covering its body. It also had a big fluffy white tail with a black stripe instead of a black tail with a white stripe. "I don't know what kind of a skunk this is, but hopefully now that it knows you live in the back yard, it will go somewhere else to live for the winter months."

The next day when I was out in my back yard, I looked for this skunk but didn't see it. I guess I really did scare it because I never saw it again. I was not aware such stinky creatures lived in the forest. I hope this funny-looking skunk never comes back, because I certainly won't miss it or the smell that it created.

After a couple of weeks of rolling in the dirt and grass of my back yard, the skunk smell on me finally was gone. I definitely won't be chasing after any more stinky varmints.

Living in the mountains of Colorado is a great education, and in a very short amount of time, I am becoming a seasoned mountain cat!

Now, instead of running around foolishly when I am out in the forest, I have become more alert. I take the time to stop, look and listen for any danger that might be present. I do this even when I am playing with or eating a varmint.

My dad said that he has noticed I have recently started being more aware, and he thinks I am a really smart cat for protecting myself against a predator attack at all times. The mountain lion kill spot that I saw a while ago made me realize I needed to pay better attention when I am out in the forest.

The warm weather didn't last long, because this morning when we went out for a walk, it was cold. The wind blew hard, and there were a couple of inches of fresh snow on the ground. Today my dad had a strange-looking device in his hands. After walking around a while in the cold fresh snow, I learned what this strange thing was when he opened it up and sat down on it. The device was a three-legged collapsible stool that he could use to sit on when there was snow on the ground.

I immediately took advantage of this and jumped on his lap so I could warm my cold paws. As I was getting warm, I thought, what a smart dad for buying this stool so we could take a break together in the cold snow. I was impressed by this new device, because I knew I would be able to warm up my paws often.

Chapter Four
THE BIG RABBIT

On the way home from our morning walk, we came down our dirt driveway, which was covered with two inches of snow. When we got to the culvert, I decided to run through it so I could temporarily warm up my cold paws. Inside the tunnel, I could smell a rabbit, and when I got to the other side I saw fresh rabbit tracks in the snow.

I decided to follow these fresh tracks, which led me to the log with the hole running through it. Now I could smell a strong scent of a rabbit and I knew I was close.

With the wind blowing so strong, I don't think the rabbit heard me coming. When I got to the end of the log, it was too late for an escape!

Instead of heading into the log where it was safe, the rabbit tried to bolt out to get away. I was excited and quickly pounced on top with all my might. I grabbed the big rabbit with all four paws and held on tightly with my claws so it couldn't get away.

This was the big rabbit that I have seen so often and because of the wind, I finally got my chance to sneak up and catch it. I grasped it up with my mouth and held on firmly with my teeth. The rabbit was as big as I was, and I could barely carry it. I knew my dad was watching me, so I headed towards him to show him what I had caught. This rabbit was so big and heavy that I had to place it down several times to rest before I reached my dad on the driveway.

I decided to share my catch with my dad, and placed the rabbit at his feet. He was completely stunned that I had caught this huge rabbit, and even more so that I wanted to share it with him. I could hear the excitement in his voice that he was very proud of what I had just accomplished. He praised me for being such a sneaky hunter, and then told me how proud he was of me for catching this elusive rabbit.

This rabbit was in such complete shock and disbelief that I had caught it, that it played dead at my dad's feet while he picked me up to hug and honor me for what I had just done. My dad was as happy as I was, and said that I was a super-cat for being able to hunt down and catch a fully-grown rabbit.

Then the rabbit noticed that we were not paying attention to it, and seized the moment to escape. It bolted up the driveway hopping as fast as it could to get back into the forest where freedom lurked.

I was so exhilarated that I didn't care that my prize had gotten away. I think that the rabbit must have felt totally relieved that it escaped unharmed.

On the way back to the house, I felt like I had a new attitude about what kind of a hunter I have become, and it showed because I had a real strut in my step! I was very excited and happy that I had finally caught this large rabbit that had eluded me on so many occasions.

I think I must have scared this rabbit so much that it decided to live somewhere else for the winter, because I didn't see it again until the following summer.

I am having a real blast hunting and exploring every day with my super cool outdoorsy kind of a dad.

He is so good to me, and I think he can read my mind because he seems to know exactly what a big kitty cat like me needs!

To get the exercise, love and attention that I never got when I was younger is a true joy, and my dad really makes me feel like a very special cat.

After all the morning excitement, I decided to go take a nap in the bedroom. I love sleeping there because it is so warm, comfortable and quiet.

I jumped up onto the down comforter and stretched out right next to the ridge that the pillow makes from being under the comforter. I fell asleep thinking about that big rabbit I had just caught.

The following morning, it was still cold outside when we went for our walk. I noticed that my dad had plowed the two inches of snow off the driveway and had shoveled the snow around the front porch and woodpile. I like it when he does this, because it keeps the freshly fallen snow from getting stuck between the pads of my paws.

I ran down the freshly plowed driveway towards the culvert, hoping I would see that big rabbit again. I did not see it, so I ran through the snow to a big pine tree so I could relieve myself.

On the way back to the house, I saw my dad sitting on the front porch talking on his phone. I headed over to the woodpile to hide. When I got near, a mouse ran out right in front of me, so I quickly caught it and started playing with it on the driveway.

After my dad finished on the phone, I noticed he was watching me skid across the frozen driveway to retrieve the mouse I was playing with.

Then he said, "Do you want to bring the mouse inside to play with it?"

I was thinking, really? He had never let me do this before. I knew exactly what he was saying because I could read his mind, and he was thinking that because it was so cold outside, it was okay to bring the mouse into the house. He held the front door open, so I quickly grabbed the mouse and headed inside.

What a super cool dad I have, allowing me to bring a mouse into the house. I enjoyed this thoroughly, because it was warm inside and I couldn't wait to play with my mouse on the soft carpet.

The mouse in the house didn't have a chance to get away, with the great traction and speed I was getting on the carpet with my claws out. It was a fast little varmint, and I enjoyed playing with it and letting it escape several times under or behind the furniture.

After getting exhausted playing with this mouse, I decided that because I was having so much fun chasing after it, I would let it go instead of eating it. Now I was sure there was a mouse in the house, and I planned on catching it again soon.

Then my dad asked me if I would like a warmed up tasty gravy snack. I meowed back, "I sure would." Because it was cold outside, my dad had started to warm up my gravy snack pouches on top of the wood burning stove. This made the gravy warm and delicious and felt really good inside my hungry belly.

My dad is the coolest dude west of the Mississippi River. How totally thoughtful of him to warm up my gravy snacks!

After wolfing down this tasty treat, I jumped onto my dad's lap to thank him for treating me so good. I could hear his heartbeat, and it sounded so soothing! I felt like I was in cat heaven and ended up taking a nap right there on his lap.

The next few weeks, the weather remained very cold outside, which shortened our daily walks into the forest. With nothing else to do, I started taking longer naps during the day to stay warm and comfortable.

The day before Christmas, the weather outside turned warmer, so my dad and I went for a long walk through the forest. We ended up in a meadow directly across from our neighbor who owned all the cats.

Chapter Five
WINTER VARMINTS

There I smelled a rabbit, so I started tracking it down. When I got close to a strong rabbit smell I got myself ready to pounce on anything that moved.

Then all of a sudden, this huge rabbit stood up on its hind legs and just looked at me. I went to chase after it, but I stopped dead in my tracks because this rabbit was three times the size of the big rabbit I had just caught a few weeks earlier. I started thinking while I was watching, could this be the same rabbit that I caught, who has now grown up to be even bigger? This rabbit was as big as a fox or a small coyote, and had ears that were about a foot long and three inches wide. It hopped around a little bit before taking off. It kept standing up on its back legs to look at my dad and I. It certainly wasn't frightened of us, and eventually it hopped away at its own pace.

I looked at my dad and he looked at me in disbelief at what we had both seen. Then he said, "I myself have never seen a rabbit that big, have you?" I meowed back, "No I haven't!"

That must have been a Colorado mountain Jackrabbit! I have heard that they were big, but I never realized that they were this big.

We were both in awe at what we were seeing, and even when this rabbit got far away from us, you could still see it clearly.

I was thinking, "Wow, what an extremely big rabbit." I'd bet the fox or the coyote would be frightened by this super big rabbit and probably couldn't catch it even if they wanted to.

I think the only predators in the forest capable of catching this super-sized rabbit would be the ferocious mountain lion or maybe the mighty eagle or the silent owl.

That evening after I went to sleep, I had a nightmare that this big rabbit was actually chasing after and trying to catch me! I woke up trembling and was sure glad I was inside, safe and sound sleeping next to my dad.

The next day I was still thinking about this tremendously-sized rabbit and how it had terrified me in my dreams.

I consider myself brave, but if I ever see that rabbit again, I think I will climb up a tree just to be safe!

Today is Christmas, and after I wolfed down my warmed-up gravy snack, my dad gave me a really cool Christmas present. It was a cardboard cat scratcher! I immediately jumped on this new toy and started sharpening my claws by scratching on it.

Then my dad put a couple tablespoons of catnip at the end of this strange-looking cardboard toy. For the first time in my life, I tried eating some catnip. This stuff smelled funny but tasted good and after a few minutes made me very relaxed and incredibly dreamy.

I ended up laying on the cardboard scratcher for hours. What was this stuff that looked like grass, smelled like tea, and made me feel very relaxed? I have to say, "I love my Christmas present and my dad."

Later, on this glorious day, I caught a mouse out in the garage while my dad was working on his truck. I brought the mouse to him and dropped it at his feet. He saw me do this and said to me, "What is this? Are you sharing your mouse snack with your dad?" I meowed back, "This is your Christmas present. Merry Christmas, dad!"

He said, "You are a cool cat and I thank you for sharing your mouse with me."

My dad and I had a good Christmas together, and in the evening we sat in front of the wood stove getting toasty while we watched an exciting adventure movie.

The next few days it remained mild, but it was still cold first thing in the morning. Three days in a row it warmed into the upper fifties. Pretty nice weather for the end of December in the mountains of Colorado.

On one of these cold mornings after our walk, I decided to hide under the clear plastic that covered the wood pile to see if I could catch a bird. I have noticed that when it is cold, the birds hide under the plastic to stay warm. My dad has the split wood stacked in rows with a space between them. With the plastic covering the wood, it makes a great hiding place for me and the birds. The plastic is held down at the ends with big rocks, and the front and back of the woodpile are open slightly because the plastic only comes down to about a foot above the ground. When there is snow on the ground it is always dry underneath.

So today when I was hiding under the plastic looking out the opening, a crazy bird didn't see me hiding there and flew right under there with me. I was happily surprised and leaped up, catching me a birdy snack. This sparrow didn't have a chance to get away, because I had it grasped firmly in my mouth. I headed out from underneath the plastic to show my dad what I had caught. He was inside, so I decided to play birdy out in the driveway.

I was very excited that I caught the bird, because they are hard to catch. In the wintertime, only the small black sparrows will stick around and brave the cold. All the other birds must head south for the winter, because I don't see them.

I wanted to play with the bird, so I let it out of my grasp hoping it would try to fly away. It played dead for a few seconds, and then quickly tried to fly away. I had my eyes on the bird, so I leaped up and retrieved it before it could flee. I did this three times before the bird got lucky and escaped.

I was so happy that I caught a bird, that I didn't care that it got away while I was playing with it. I knew I would get another chance because these sparrows lived nearby and landed in the driveway every morning to eat small rocks that helps with their digestive systems.

I see these birds every day and I have tried to catch them on several occasions. Apparently, these birds know that I live here, because whenever they see me hanging out by the front porch or wood pile they will always land just far enough away from me so I can't catch them.

So I got smart and started hiding under the plastic or the front porch so they couldn't see me.

I think the reason that the bird family braves landing close to me is because they need the small rocks for their digestive system, and our dirt driveway has lots of them. After my dad plows the driveway, the sun melts away any remaining snow which offers the birds what they desire. Amazingly, the sun hits this area on the driveway right by the wood pile and the front porch early in the morning. That is why the birds come here for their rocks rather than somewhere else.

Because there is not much else to hunt right now, I have been spending a lot of my time trying to catch another one of these sparrows. Now that they can't see me when I am hiding, I have noticed that the whole bird family has been landing closer to me, not realizing the danger that they are really in.

After they land, they run around collecting small rocks, sometimes within a foot or two of my hiding place. It is just a matter of time before I catch another one of these birds again.

Then one really cold morning, my dad was sitting on the front porch drinking his coffee while I was hiding under the plastic waiting for the bird family to land. After they landed, I watched them scurry around collecting rocks in the driveway.

The birds couldn't see me hiding by the woodpile, and eventually two of them came within inches of the opening under the plastic. I felt so excited that these birds were close, that I crouched down and prepared to attack. Then, like a bolt of lightning, I sprinted forward and leaped up to catch one of these daring birds. I think they were a bit frozen, because they didn't fly away as fast as they usually did.

My dad saw me catch the bird in mid-air from his view on the front porch. Then he said, "Your silent attack looked awesome. What a fast, sneaky super-cat you are!"

I was very happy that all the hard work I put in hiding, finally paid off. I went out into the middle of the driveway and quickly devoured this birdy snack.

Birds are hard to catch, especially in the wintertime. I felt boldly smart for using my cunningness to catch another one of these birds. Once again I had a real strut in my step, and I decided to savor this moment before I searched around the front yard for something else to catch.

Chapter Six
THE NEW YEAR

Today my dad and I are celebrating the arrival of a new year inside our house. Last night over a foot of fresh snow fell, and when he opened the front door I couldn't believe how much snow was piled up on the front porch. I was thinking, "I'm not going out there!" After my dad shoveled off the front porch, I went around the steps and under the porch where it was dry. I searched around, hoping to find a mouse or rabbit hiding under there.

I was curious about all this snow that we had gotten last night, and I wondered how I was going to get from the porch over to the woodpile. I built up my courage and thought that if I ran really fast, maybe I could plow my way through the deep snow to the woodpile.

Then you could say curiosity got the cat, because I needed to know if I could make it through this cold deep white stuff. About halfway between the porch and the woodpile, I realized that running through the snow wasn't going to work. Snow was getting in my eyes and ears, so I started jumping up and over this incredibly cold challenge. When I got to the woodpile, the snow was so deep, there was no longer an opening between the ground and the plastic covering the wood. I had to dig in the snow to get under the plastic where it was safe and dry.

I almost got stuck in the snow when I tried to run from the porch over to the woodpile. It was up to my ears and very cold.

My dad must have read my mind, because he shoveled the snow from the porch over to where I was hiding. What a relief, seeing him and a freshly-shoveled path back to the house. He said, "You must have some hound dog blood in you! You looked like a powder hound running through the snow!"

It was pure joy heading back to the house on a shoveled path. I sat on the front porch and watched my dad struggle to shovel that deep snow. Then I realized this stuff was too deep to go outside to find a spot, and I would have to use my litter box for the first time ever!

My dad said that after he shoveled and plowed the snow, he would take me out for a walk. When we did go, we had to stay on the freshly plowed driveway because the snow was too deep to run anywhere else. This was the first time that I have ever seen so much snow, and it was quite exhilarating. I now had to wonder, how do the mice, rabbits and chipmunks get around with the snow so deep?

Over the next couple of weeks, our daily walks were shortened and we were confined to the driveway or the main dirt road we lived on. The only thing I saw to hunt was the bird family.

Winter was here with its short days and long, cold nights. With very little hunting to do, life seemed kind of boring. The only enjoyment we were getting was sitting in front of the wood stove, watching a movie or eating something tasty.

It was the third week in January, and even though it has been cold outside, the intense Colorado sun at this elevation has melted away most of the snow. I can't wait till winter is over so I can get back to doing some hunting. I have missed sneaking around terrifying the varmint population.

The only thing that has been good about winter is the extra time I get to spend with my super cool dad. He doesn't work as much in the winter time, and hangs out around the house more often.

Since I have been adopted, my dad and I have become such good friends that we are able to share a very special bond between us that I never thought was possible between a man and a cat. The way we can read each other's mind is unbelievably cool and my love for him is truly immeasurable!

It is pure joy waking up every day knowing that my dad loves me enough to spend time with me, playing with me or taking me outside for walks. It makes the long winter days go by quickly and I enjoy his company.

It sure beats sleeping all day or being stuck in a motorhome with people who know nothing about cats.

My dad made me a new toy to play with. It is a stuffed cloth mouse hooked to a long string, that is attached to a short stick. Now we can play mouse in the house, and to do this my dad will put a blanket in the middle of the living room floor and puff it up to make it look bigger.

Then as I am watching, he pulls the mouse behind the blanket with the stick and string to make it hide. When he does this quickly, it makes the cloth mouse look real, and that excites me into attacking it. Then I will run across the carpet and slam into the blanket while I reach under it to try and snag the cloth mouse.

It is fun playing mouse in the house, and the extra exercise I am getting certainly makes up for our shortened daily walks.

Another thing that my dad does to stimulate my response to attack is he will hide the mouse around the corner of a wall or piece of furniture and then he will quickly pull it into sight and across the carpet.

Then I will attack by sprinting across the carpet and sliding on my side with my paw extended to snag up this fast-moving cloth mouse. After I vigorously grab it up, I will roll over onto my back, tossing it up into the air and then catching it again!

I am having a blast playing with this new toy, and I think it is improving my reaction time. This spring and summer I will be even faster than before, so the varmints better watch out.

Today when we woke up, it was sunny and gorgeous outside. It must be in the sixties, which is truly amazing for the end of January. My dad was heading out back to hang his wet laundry on the clothesline, so I followed him. Within minutes of being out there, I located and caught another mouse under the back porch.

Then I noticed that big dad was done hanging his laundry and was heading back inside. I quickly followed him with the mouse in my mouth. There was still snow on the ground, so I thought playing with this mouse on the carpet would be better. I don't think my dad saw the mouse as we headed inside, and I knew he wouldn't care even if he did. He seemed pleasantly surprised when he saw me playing with it on the carpet, and I was feeling pure joy being able to do so.

This was a medium-sized mouse, and after playing with it for a while I decided this mouse was going to be a tasty snack, so I ate it.

I am still thinking about the mouse I let go in the house a couple of weeks ago. I am going to get up in the middle of the night and track this varmint down so I can catch it again.

Today was February first, and only a trace of snow was left on the north-facing slopes. With the snow almost gone, we are once again able to walk in any direction through the forest to take our daily walks. I like going to different places every day because it increases my chances of catching something, and it keeps our walks interesting.

There is a small cabin with a front porch located at the top of our dirt driveway. The people who had the house built, lived in this cabin until the house was finished. I have seen rabbit tracks in the snow around the cabin, and I have smelled the rabbit by a hole that goes under it. So this morning, I led my dad up the driveway to the cabin to see if I could find that stinky long-eared rabbit. There is a four-foot fence that surrounds it, and some days I will wait for my dad to open up the gate to look for this rabbit. Today I decided to jump over the fence at one corner that has a wooden rail on top. I wanted to try and surprise the rabbit before my dad got close with his noisy boots. I did not see or smell it today, so I searched around the cabin for a chipmunk or a mouse.

The cabin has a porch with four wooden poles that supports the front of the porch roof that covers it. The back side of this roof is slightly higher and is attached to the cabin. Three of the support poles are cut off, so that the roof rests on top of them. The fourth pole is not cut off and extends above and up the side of this roof about a foot.

Today I was feeling a bit rambunctious, so I sharpened my claws at the bottom of the pole and then I climbed all the way to the top of this eight-foot pole. Then I jumped down one foot to the porch roof. I looked around for a while, before I jumped up two feet onto the main roof.

At the top of the roof I could see my dad open up the gate to the fence and walk alongside the cabin. He noticed me standing up there and said, "How did you get up there, you crazy cat?"

This was the first time I have been up on this roof, and I felt very proud that I figured out how to do that. I looked down upon my dad and gave him a little meow saying, "I am a smart cat, that's how!"

Then, after looking around the main roof and checking out the view from up there, I jumped back down onto the porch roof. I was kind of stuck up there because I was now seven feet off the ground with no simple way down.

Going down the pole I climbed up was going to be harder, because the pole was smooth and slippery and didn't have any branches to slow me down.

I could hear my dad standing on the porch down below, and hoped that he was reading my mind, that I wanted to jump down onto his back to get off the roof.

Sure enough, he must have read my mind because he walked off the porch to the corner of the roof where it was the lowest. He saw me sitting up there, and asked me if I needed some help. Then as he stood slightly away from the corner of the roof, he bent over with his arms out to make his back bigger, to give me more room to jump down.

I now had a three-foot jump down from the roof to his back. As he stood still, I jumped down onto this platform he offered me. I trusted my dad completely, and knew his back would be a soft place to land. After I safely landed, I jumped down from his back and felt exhilarated that he had helped me again out of a difficult situation. I love my dad!

Then he told me I am an unbelievably smart, brave cat and that he couldn't believe I was crazy enough to be up on the roof exploring. "What a strong, amazing cat!"

I love that my dad talks to me, and even more so that I understand what he is saying. I do feel brave, and a little crazy living high in the mountains and having all this room to roam and hunt. What a lucky cat I am to have such an incredible dad.

We live on twenty acres of treed land that borders the Pike National Forest. Occasionally my dad takes me on long walks into this vast and dangerous place. Being able to explore this wild terrain has made me the brave cat that I am.

Staying close to my dad on these long walks gives me the courage to prowl and hunt this unknown wilderness.

Big dad said he was told by one of our neighbors that there is a family of twenty or more mountain lions that live and hunt in these woods. There are also several coyote packs that do the same. I have heard them crying out when they are chasing something to eat, and I have heard them howling during the full moon. When they are close by, the sound of a coyote pack is very frightening and always makes me want to climb up a tree to feel safe.

I think my dad enjoys the great outdoors as much as I do, and I am glad he comes with me to keep me company and watch my back.

On one of our walks through the Pike National Forest it was early morning, when we saw a pair of gray wolves prowling and hunting together. When I first saw them, I was startled because they were so close and we were out in the middle of an opening with no big trees nearby to climb.

I was glad my dad was with me, because these wolves were big and looked very hungry.

Then my dad did something that I had never seen him do before. He started chasing after them with his big noisy boots. Now the wolves were startled, and immediately started to run in the opposite direction. Even after they took off running and weren't a threat anymore, big dad kept running towards them. They both kept looking over their shoulders in disbelief that my dad was still chasing after them. They started running even faster, and soon disappeared into the forest.

When my dad came back to find me, I was in awe of what he had just done. I was certainly glad he wasn't chasing after me, because the noise he was making running after those wolves definitely was scary, and kind of frightened me. I couldn't imagine the fear those wolves were feeling being chased by big dad. I bet they will never get that close to a human again!

What a brave dad I have, trying to protect me against these sneaky, cunning predators.

After the scare and adrenalin rush subsided, my dad and I headed off into the forest towards a tall pyramid-shaped mountain. You could see it sticking up off in the distance. I was excited, because I could read my dad's mind that he wanted to hike up there and check it out. He was also thinking that he wasn't sure if I would make it all the way to the top.

I love my dad and all the time that he spends with me every day. Sometimes on the weekends we will go for walks that last three to four hours. It is a total blast going exploring and hanging out with big dad.

It didn't take us very long to reach the top. Being a young buckaroo, I was full of energy, and even though this little mountain was really steep, it didn't tire me out. I had to wait several times for dad, who was forced to catch his breath.

The view was awesome, and there was a slight warming wind blowing out of the south. My dad was so proud of me for making it all the way to the top. I could hear it in his voice. He picked me up and gave me a big hug and a kiss. Then he told me that he was really impressed that I made it all the way to the top, because this was the farthest that we had ever been away from the house!

I felt very lucky and proud as my dad held me. He slowly turned in a circle so we could see the incredible view. Being on top of this pyramid mountain with my dad was truly exhilarating. I felt so incredibly loved and happy, that my whole body was vibrating intensely because I was purring so hard!

After a while, I was placed back down on the ground so my dad could sit down and rest on his three-legged collapsible stool.

Then big dad did something that surprised me. He had thought ahead to bring us a snack and some water.

Out of his coat pocket, he pulled two sandwich bags and a container of water. One of the bags had a handful of my crunchy giblet cat food, and the other bag big dad rolled up to make a small bowl to hold my drinking water.

I was really thirsty, and had my head in the sandwich bag, drinking before he could fill it full with water. After eating and drinking, I sat down to take a break with my dad.

It felt like spring was near because the days were getting warmer. The wind that blew out of the south was always warmer than the wind out of the north. Today the wind was blowing just strong enough to tickle my whiskers!

After resting for about twenty minutes, my dad asked me if I was ready to head back to the house. I meowed back, "Yes I am!"

Going down this steep little mountain was definitely harder and more treacherous than going up. Big dad was going slow, and I had to wait for him a few times to catch up.

When we got down off the mountain and back into the dense forest, I found a tree that had fallen over onto another. It rested at about a thirty-degree angle and was about a foot in diameter, with very few branches down near the ground.

I dashed up this fallen tree to check out the view. When I got near the top, I could smell the scent of a squirrel.

I looked around and soon located the squirrel escaping to a nearby tree. It is amazing how fast they can leap through the air to another waiting tree branch.

I am fast, but I haven't learned how to fly yet!

When my dad walked under the fallen tree, he told me he could see me hiding up there. I felt extremely excited, so I ran down the tree and exploded across the forest floor as fast as I could run. I made it to a rock outcropping and jumped up onto it, where I waited for my dad.

He walked over and kissed me on my head while gently squeezing my back. Then he said, "I have never seen you so fired up!"

I was feeling very happy and overly excited spending the entire morning roaming around with my big dad. I am truly the luckiest cat west of the Mississippi River.

With spring just weeks away, I couldn't wait to see something to catch and get back to some serious hunting. This year I am bigger, stronger, faster and smarter than I was last year, so I think I will be more successful catching many more varmints. I am downright excited!

Chapter Seven
THE BOND AT CASTLE RIDGE

I can tell spring has finally arrived because the birds are chirping and the weather is starting to get really nice. The days are warmer, but the nights and mornings are still chilly.

Today is Saturday, and after our morning walk in paradise, I sensed that my dad was going somewhere in his truck.

Only thing was, I didn't know that I was going with him until later.

I was still frightened by the sound of his truck and was afraid to go in it for fear of being taken back to kitty jail! Whenever my dad's truck was in the driveway, I always stayed clear of it for these reasons.

This morning my dad fooled me by picking me up to give me a hug. As he was holding me, I could read his mind that something was up. He was going somewhere in his truck, so I tried to escape his grasp and jump down.

He held onto me as he climbed into his truck. Then he told me not to worry, that he was taking me to a special spot to go for another walk.

I was excited and a little frightened as he closed the door and started up the Toyota truck. This was the first time I had been in my dad's truck since I was adopted.

Then as we drove down the driveway, I started to feel better when big dad rolled down the driver's side window so I could get some fresh air. I immediately jumped on his lap and stuck my head out the window.

My dad held me against his chest with his left arm, to hold me firmly so I wouldn't jump out.

I had my front paws on the truck door armrest, and my rear paws securely on his lap.

This enabled me to stick my head out the window while I was comfortably supported.

The air blowing past my snout was exhilarating, and all the new smells were delightful!

This wasn't so bad riding in my dad's truck. I truly enjoy hanging out with him.

Soon we drove past our neighbor's house. They have several horses that like to stand close to the road while grazing in the pasture. I recognized their smell and made eye contact with them briefly.

I was having fun on this new adventure and when we reached the tar road, big dad rolled up the window. We started going really fast and everything looked like a blur.

He told me not to worry and that we would be to this new spot soon.

I was feeling dizzy, so I sat down on the seat and rested my body against his legs while I waited patiently.

There was this unbelievable loud noise that the wind made, blowing past dad's truck. I felt scared because my ears were whistling.

It wasn't long before we slowed down and turned onto another dirt road. This one had more bumps on it and we had to go really slow.

I took my position back on my dad's lap as he rolled down the window.

I felt very excited as we ventured into the forest to find a new place to roam.

After awhile, dad stopped the truck and opened up the door so I could jump out.

We were definitely in a new spot that we had never been to before. Big dad grabbed the three-legged collapsible stool, the water, and some snacks and then asked me if I was ready to go for a walk. I meowed back, "Yes I am!"

Dad let me lead the way, so off we went into the forest. Immediately, we came to a steep slope that led us down to a deer trail. I followed this trail until we reached the bottom of this ravine.

Straight ahead, I could see this huge rock pile that looked like a castle.

My dad said to me, "I thought you would like this spot."

These rocks looked like a good place to hunt chipmunks. I was very happy and couldn't wait to climb up on these steep rocks to play and hunt.

I felt so strong that I immediately jumped up four feet, to the top of this boulder. When I looked up this rocky ridge, I saw two chipmunks scurrying away.

With my dad following, I prowled after these noisy chipmunks.

It did not take these varmints long to realize that I was in pursuit.

They started screaming out their warning sounds alerting every chipmunk in the area.

As I was sneaking close, this one chipmunk sat bravely on top of this rock and watched me as I approached.

I was hoping it wouldn't move as I leaped up to catch this elusive varmint.

Unfortunately, it had already vanished when I landed. I looked around and saw three other chipmunks running away. I felt I was in chipmunk heaven as I scurried after them.

The rocks and boulders were steep and offered the chipmunks good hiding places. When I got near the top of the ridge, I located one of these noisy chipmunks hiding under a boulder.

My dad finally caught up to me, high up on the ridge. He saw that I was hunting something, so he asked me if I needed some help. I meowed back, "I sure do!"

It always amazes me that my dad can climb over these large rocks and boulders as good as I can. He always seems to keep up despite his age.

Big dad is so smart in the way he helps me hunt. He saw the hole that I was sitting by and knowingly went to the other side of this boulder to try and scare this noisy chipmunk my way.

He blew into the hole under this rock several times, but nothing came out. My dad had scared this chipmunk into being quiet, and after waiting for a while, I realized it wasn't coming out to play.

When we got to the top of this rocky ridge that looked like a castle, we came to a natural trail that ran the length of it from north to south. This ridge wasn't as wide as it was long and stood about 800 feet above the valley floors that lingered down below.

With my dad following close, I headed down this trail towards the north.

I was feeling very excited and couldn't wait to explore this entire rock. Along the way, I heard something move to my left so I jumped up to the top of the rocks that stood about seven feet above the trail. There I saw a rabbit trying to escape. I quickly disappeared from my dad's view, in hot pursuit of this elusive varmint. I soon came to a small hole under some rocks located next to a cliff. This rabbit had built its home in an awesome spot and I could smell and hear it hiding in there.

After checking out the view from the rabbit's doorstep, I looked up to notice my dad watching me from above.

I quickly jumped from one boulder to another and joined back up with him.

I could read his mind and he was entertained by my speed and strength.

Then he said to me, "It is really cool watching you jump from rock to rock."

I was happy that he had noticed how strong I felt and how quickly I navigated the rocks to reach him.

We continued down this trail together, heading north. When we came to the end of the trail, it had a 700-foot drop-off on all three sides. There was quite a view, so my dad sat down on the rocks to check it out.

I immediately jumped up onto my dad's lap in appreciation. After receiving a big hug, I started exploring the nose of this cliff-like structure.

The view was awesome and I was feeling very brave standing on the edge of this new and exciting spot.

I was so glad that my dad had fooled me into riding in his truck so he could take me on this new adventure to this awesome ridge.

I was having a blast checking everything out and just couldn't stay still for very long.

Down below I could see three mule deer grazing in a meadow. I don't think that they could see us because only our heads were visible to them.

* * *

I heard my dad call for me as he headed back down the ridge trail to the south. I quickly joined up with him so I could lead the way. I love my dad and how he always waits for me to catch up.

Then, up ahead, I saw another long-eared stinky rabbit.

I quickly prowled its way, hoping I would get a chance to use my new and improved speed and strength to catch me a rabbit!

This rabbit was prepared and when it saw me coming, it bolted down the rocky ridge with impressive speed.

All I could do is watch as it quickly disappeared in the boulders down below.

There were rabbits and chipmunks everywhere! My dad had found us a really good hunting spot.

I was having a blast exploring, and down the trail a little farther, I saw a squirrel sitting in a tree.

I didn't think it saw me coming, so I sprinted up this tree to get closer.

Well, that frightened this squirrel big time! It ran up to a top branch, and started chattering loudly at me. It was watching me as I climbed up a little further.

I was now thinking, "I got this squirrel boxed in." There was no way past me, and I was completely ready if it tried to.

I was almost near the top of this tree, and this squirrel was getting frantic.

It was making an incredible amount of noise and moving its tail up and down while looking straight at me.

We were having a stare down and when I decided to move up one more branch to get closer, this crazy squirrel sprinted across this upper branch and leaped twenty feet through the air to a waiting limb of another tree.

I was surprised that this squirrel had managed to escape. I never knew that a squirrel could fly that far. Simply unbelievable!

As I was descending, I noticed that my dad had been watching me. He said, "Good try, you brave cat!"

When I got near the bottom, my dad let me jump down onto his shoulders.

It was such a nice day with the sun shining brightly. I was truly having fun hanging out with my dad.

Then, big dad sat down on his three-legged collapsible stool, and pulled out the snacks and the water.

We hung out in the shade of this pine tree that I was just hunting in for a short time until I finished my snacks and water.

I love that my dad talks to me often and how he seems to understand me! I also like how he has been bringing us water and food on all of our walks.

After our little break, we headed down the ridge trail to the south. I was very alert and soon saw another chipmunk scurrying away.

The ridge we were on was now only about 50 feet high, with grassy meadows on both sides.

I went running after this noisy chipmunk, who quickly vanished into an opening under this big rock. When I got to this opening, I realized the hole under the rock was big enough for me to fit inside.

I needed to investigate this little cave, so I looked back at my dad for approval before I headed inside to see what I could find.

This was more than just a hole under a rock. It was a cave that went in several feet to a larger chamber.

My eyes were starting to adjust to the low light, which made it possible for me to see where I was going.

I could smell the chipmunk I had been chasing and started exploring to see if I could locate it.

I was impressed with my new discovery and thought this cave would be a good hiding spot.

There was no sign of the chipmunk, so I decided to sit down inside the big chamber to listen for anything that might move.

A little while later, I heard my dad say, "Where did you go, you crazy cat?"

I soon realized that he could not see me resting inside this dark cave. I could hear him walking around outside, and then amazingly, he stuck his head into the opening and said, "Are you in there, Lucky?"

I waited a few moments and then meowed back, "Yes I am!"

Then, for the first time ever, I heard my meow echo through the cave. I did not know what to think. Was this another cat, or was this noise just me?

After resting peacefully inside my new hideout, I peeked my head out to see what my dad was up to.

He was happily sitting on a rock waiting for me.

A hawk was flying above, so I ventured out to see what it was hunting.

After leaving the cave, I realized that this would be a safe place to hide if it rained, snowed, or if a predator was trying to get me.

The opening for this cave was just big enough for me to fit though, and would keep out anything bigger. What a cool place I had found!

I started to wonder if there were other dark caves lurking about. I looked around for a while but didn't find any more.

My dad was still waiting for me, resting on his three-legged collapsible stool, so I jumped up onto his lap. He gave me a big hug and told me that he loved me.

The bond and love that I was feeling for my dad was truly immeasurable!

A couple of hours had passed before big dad asked me if I was ready to go home. I was thinking 'not really', but if you say so!

As we slowly headed back, I started thinking about riding in dad's truck. I was still scared of cars and trucks, so I started having second thoughts about getting close to my dad's truck. He kind of fooled me before we left, but now that I knew we were leaving in the truck, I chickened out!

When we got near, I turned around and quickly started heading back towards the rocky ridge.

My dad yelled at me, "It's time to go!"

I was thinking, go ahead, I am staying.

He started running after me saying, "Let's go, Lucky-Son-Jones."

I had a good head start and started running even faster to keep well ahead of him.

Big dad ran after me all the way back to the bottom of the ravine.

I jetted into the grey rocks of the castle ridge, where I was completely camouflaged.

After hiding, I could hear my dad breathing hard. He was swearing about how he had hurt his right knee chasing after me. It was obvious that he was in pain because he was moaning and grunting.

A little while later, I heard my dad say to me, "I am going back to the truck. Are you coming?"

I chose to stay silent as I hid among the rocks.

I heard my dad grunting in pain as he slowly walked back to the top of the slope. He called for me to come one more time before he disappeared over the horizon.

As I sat there hiding, I wasn't sure what to think. I knew that big dad was kind of mad at me for running away, but would he abandon me like my previous owners?

I started to wonder if I could make it on my own, out here in the wilderness. I could stay in the cave I had found, but where would I get food and water?

Then I started to think about my incredible dad. I truly loved him and would miss him dearly if I never saw him again.

An empty feeling came over me and I started to worry. About twenty-five minutes or more had passed, and there was no sign of my dad.

I was now paralyzed with worry. Thoughts of abandonment went racing through my mind. Would my dad of six months leave me out here in the forest? Who would ever love me as much as he does? Who would hug and talk to me?

I felt like I couldn't move and started to feel really sad.

Then, I heard a noise coming my way. I listened closely and soon realized it was the grunting, moaning sound of my dad walking. I could read his mind and he was worried about me.

He was out looking for me, even though he had hurt his knee.

When he got to the bottom of the ravine where he had last seen me, he called out for me.

I was glad to hear the sound of his voice and was extremely happy that he had come back to rescue me.

I immediately meowed back to let him know that I was all right.

I could hear it in his voice how relieved he was that I didn't run off.

He called for me again in a very loving way, and once again I meowed back to let him know exactly where I was.

Big dad walked toward the sound of my meows until he found me.

After he picked me up and gave me a super-big hug, I could feel and sense how much he loved me.

I was so happy that he didn't abandon me.

Then, I read his mind and discovered that he was overwhelmed with joy that he had found me. He was also thinking that I must really love him because I could have taken off and never seen him again.

He held onto me as we walked back to the truck. I was still

reading his mind and he was thinking how smart it was of me to meow back, letting him know exactly where I was.

Big dad was also thinking about a new name for me. From now on, he was going to refer to me as his "Royal-Psychic-Super Cat".

He thought I looked like royalty with my unique white fur markings. He knew I was telepathic because I could read his mind and he thought I was super because I was very smart and could talk to him.

The ride home was less frightening than I thought and after getting home, I started to imagine going to other places in big dad's truck.

Chapter Eight
THE ENDLESS SUMMER

Spring is here and summer is near. I am now one-and-a-half years old and I have been feeling excited about being bigger, faster, and stronger.

I am ready to do some hunting and I'm up to the challenge. The local varmints better watch out!

Today, on our morning walk, it was sunny and warm. I was feeling pumped up, so I decided to check out my new and improved claw strength.

I have been keeping my claws razor-sharp by using my cardboard cat scratcher and the sides of big trees.

Along the way, I saw this big pine tree with large, low-lying branches. These branches were five inches in diameter and were only about three feet above the ground. This pine tree had lots of branches and stood about sixty feet tall.

I looked back at my dad to see if he was watching.

Then, with impressive speed and strength, I leaped from a standstill, up three-and-a-half feet, to one of these waiting branches.

After landing, I ran up about eight feet along this open branch, towards the thick trunk. This was a big tree that had lots of thick branches jetting out all around it at seemingly the perfect height for me to jump up higher and higher.

Within seconds, I was fifty feet off the ground. These wide branches really made it safe for me to climb.

I was feeling brave and very secure with my super-strong claws. I looked down to see if big dad was still watching.

This was the highest I had ever gotten myself up in any tree and it was quite exhilarating.

I started checking out the view from way up here and noticed that there weren't any chipmunks or squirrels up this high.

The view was great, so I jumped up even higher. I was now sixty-five feet off the ground, so I started strutting my stuff and scratching on this super-high tree branch that I was resting on.

As I was checking out the view, I heard my dad say to me, "Lucky-Son-Jones, how are you going to get down out of that tree?" I stared at him and while I looked him in the eyes, I meowed, saying, "I will be right down."

I was feeling exhilarated, brave, and very strong. Without hesitation, I jumped down one branch at a time, slowly navigating my way around the tree trunk counter-clockwise, until I was just above my dad's head.

He was standing down there waiting for me and then asked me if I wanted to jump down onto his back.

After jumping down onto his shoulders, I started rubbing my head against his in appreciation.

It feels so good to truly be loved by my dad. I decided to ride around on his shoulders to be close to him. Then, up ahead, I saw something move.

Big dad sensed that I wanted down, so he leaned back and held out his right knee, to give me a safe place to jump down.

I swear my dad is telepathic and can read my mind. That is exactly what I was thinking and that knee trick worked perfectly to get me down safely.

I quickly ran ahead to see what I could find. There, straight ahead was a small black squirrel. I went racing after it, but it saw me coming, and escaped to a nearby tree.

I then decided to hide behind this tree while I waited for my dad to walk by. When he got close, I raced out from behind this tree to surprise him.

He was startled, and reached down to touch my tail as I raced by. Then he said to me, "What are you doing, you crazy cat?"

I was feeling fired up, so I went over to where my dad was standing and reached up his left leg as far as I could. I then sank my claws into the material of his pants and hung there briefly, while stretching myself out.

It is really cool that a big dad lets me do this without getting mad. Luckily, my dad wears long johns – thermal underwear – underneath his pants, which keeps my claws from digging into his skin.

I like the feeling of hanging in midair, while I am stretching. What a cool dad I have!

* * *

On the way back to the house, I found an animal trail going up this hill. I decided to follow it to see where it went. The local deer make most of these trails and I could smell their scent as I ventured up this path.

When I got to the top of the ridge on this trail, I saw a baby rabbit hiding next to a large boulder.

I crouched down and started prowling close, hoping I could catch it.

Then, out of nowhere and as fast as a bolt of lightning, this big hawk soared down from high above and tried to grab me.

Big dad was watching and leaped forward to scare away this hungry hawk.

I was certainly thankful that my dad was watching my back, because he surely saved my life!

Apparently, this large hawk was sitting high above in a tree being very stealth, waiting for a chance to catch this baby rabbit.

I think that this hawk wasn't very happy about me interfering with his morning hunting session, so it tried to attack me.

After learning about this new threat that lurked in the trees, I became more aware of my surroundings. I kept my eyes focused all around, including up above me every time we were out in the forest.

When we got home, my dad let me out into the backyard. I immediately went on patrol to see what I could find.

As I was hiding in the long grass, I noticed my dad come out into the backyard, holding a blanket. He went over to one of the sheds and knelt down by an opening that went under it.

This shed stood on cinderblocks and was about one foot off the ground in the front and two-an-a-half foot in the rear.

The lower section was surrounded with chicken wire and it had only one entrance, big enough for me to fit in!

The mountain grasses had grown tall over the years and had enclosed this area, making it a safe hiding place for me to be camouflaged and hunt.

I started to read my dad's mind and learned that he had seen me hiding under there on several occasions. He was putting this blanket under the shed to give me a comfortable place to lay or nap.

I was impressed with what my dad had just done. As soon as he walked away, I went to check out my new bed under the shed.

He was right, I did spend a lot of time hiding under there, totally camouflaged and waiting in ambush for something to move.

Now under the shed, there was a really soft blanket, folded in layers and placed in my favorite place to hide. I laid down and was completely tickled how comfy I was.

This is going to be a great place to take a nap on a hot summer afternoon!

I started thinking how lucky I was being a Colorado mountain cat and having all these unique places to hide in and around my backyard. I was so happy, comfy, and delighted that I fell asleep.

After a while, I was awakened by the sound of a mouse running by. I opened up one eye and could see a mouse standing close, looking back at me! I was too relaxed to move, so I decided to hunt it down later.

I can hear everything around me and with the tall grasses that surround the shed, it makes me feel like I am in the jungle.

The smell of the spring flowers and grasses gives the forest a unique aroma, that is very pleasing to my senses!

After waking up from my nap, I rested peacefully on my new blanket, while I joyfully hunted.

Then I heard my dad calling my name. I was very curious, so I headed his way.

When I reached him, he had a handful of tasty, crunchy cat snacks that he had placed on the ground in front of me.

After I started eating, my dad started brushing my fur. I felt so excited, that my tail started shaking violently.

Big dad says that I have some snake blood in me, and that's why my tail shakes when I am excited.

On another occasion, after hearing my dad open up a can of cat food (a sound that is unmistakable!), I jumped up onto the countertop to investigate. I could smell the delicious flavor of fish.

One of the cupboard doors was open and I was so excited about getting some tasty canned food, that my tail started shaking. I was standing right next to this open door, and my vibrating tail was banging against it, producing a sound that sounded like a rattlesnake!

That was the first time that my dad had commented to me that he thought I had some snake blood in me. Crazy dad!

I love that I get brushed often, and how soft it makes my fur.

After being brushed, I watched my dad hang up this funny-looking red thing with a water container above it.

I wasn't sure what it was, so I read my dad's mind and discovered that it was a hummingbird feeder.

Then I started thinking, "What is a hummingbird?"

I love birds and couldn't wait for one to come and feed so I could see it.

Amazingly, a few days later, one showed up. I heard its chirping whistle, well before it landed on this red thing to feed.

I watched intensely, while I tried to figure out how to catch it.

Unfortunately, big dad hung this bird feeder out of my reach.

After watching this bird come and go several times, I noticed that it did sound to me like it was indeed humming while it was feeding.

Most of the time, these little colorful birds never landed or drank for very long.

After about a week went by, several other noisy, singing hummingbirds had found this new watering hole.

These birds flew in and out with amazing speed without ever flying into each other.

They seem to be communicating their whereabouts to each other with all their chirping and whistling as they came and went.

It was mesmerizing watching them fly in and out at such great speeds, as I sat there close by, just out of reach!

I was becoming discouraged, so I headed off to my cat fort for a nap.

As I tried to fall asleep, I could hear those noisy hummingbirds flying in and out at an alarming rate.

It sounded like more of these noisy birds had found the watering hole, or maybe they figured out I wasn't watching them anymore.

As I was trying to fall asleep, I was thinking, "Thanks, dad, for putting up that noisy bird feeder."

Finally, I fell asleep and dreamed about how I was going to catch me a hummingbird!

Throughout the summer, these noisy birds came and went like they owned the place.

I was certainly happy when these hummingbirds, and their noise, headed south for the winter.

The peace and quiet was exhilarating!

Today after our daily walk, I noticed big dad loading up the truck with food, water, and camping supplies.

I immediately read his mind and found out that he was taking me camping with him to this awesome spot near Lake George, Colorado.

I was excited because I could read his mind, that there was this huge rocky ridge that jutted out of nowhere!

He had been there before, many years ago and thought that I

would love to climb on these rocks and boulders because they were so steep and high.

We drove in the Toyota truck for about forty minutes before we came to a forest road. After driving in the forest for another five miles, we came to this camping spot with the large rock outcropping. I could see these rocks standing high above us as we approached, and couldn't wait to go explore.

Dad parked the truck and grabbed the three-legged collapsible stool, the water, and the snacks.

I was excited and eager to go find me a varmint to catch.

With big dad following, I headed towards a ridge of rocks that ran south away from the huge rock pile.

This ridge was about twenty feet high and ten feet across.

As soon as we got close, I saw my first chipmunk.

I darted forward in hot pursuit of this little, noisy varmint.

After hunting around this ridge for about an hour, I chased a chipmunk under a rock several times. It seemed like it wanted to play hide and seek with me, so I happily did.

My dad sat there and watched me hunt for a while, before he

said to me that he had to go set up the tent and get the camp ready.

He said I could continue to hunt and that he would be right over there.

I was excited that he was going to leave me here so I could finish playing with this brave little chipmunk.

While I was hunting, I could hear big dad setting up the camp. He had this blue tent put up in no time. I could see it clearly from where I was hunting and started thinking I couldn't wait to go explore this new fabric enclosure.

As I patiently and quietly waited, this brave little chipmunk darted out from beneath this boulder. Apparently, it did not think I was still outside waiting for it. I seized the moment and leaped on top of this fast-moving varmint.

I soon realized that this was not the same varmint that I had been playing with.

The varmint that I had just caught was a ground squirrel that was three times the size of the little chipmunk I was chasing.

I was impressed with my strength and speed as I quickly killed my first big varmint of the year.

Then, while I was tasting this new varmint, my dad amazingly appeared.

He couldn't believe that I had already caught something. I could hear it in his voice how proud he was of me.

Soon afterwards, we headed back to our new camp spot for a drink.

I was intrigued with this new tent and how the wind seemingly blew right through it.

This tent was designed to have a vehicle back into one side, with a sleeve that surrounded the body, to keep out the bugs and rain.

I jumped from the tent up into the back of the Toyota truck to see what dad had done. He had turned the entire back of the truck into a really comfy bed.

In one spot, he made it extra comfortable for me to sleep by placing a winter coat over the couch cushions in one of the corners. This coat had a silk lining and was cool to lay on.

After checking it all out, I was impressed with my dad's ability to build us a fort out in the wilderness!

After getting snacked up, I read my dad's mind and he was getting things ready for us to hike to the top of this steep rocky ridge that just seemed to jut out of nowhere. I watched him load up his coat with food and water. He had the collapsible three-legged stool and the flashlight close by.

When we go for walks, big dad uses the weight of this big flashlight, placed through a loop handle of the stool, to counterbalance it while it rests on his right shoulder. This way, he doesn't have to carry his stool and flashlight with his hands.

Soon afterwards, my dad asked me if I was ready to go do some rock climbing. I meowed back, "I sure am!"

So, instinctively I led the way, heading towards the rocky ridge. A short while later, we came to a very steep rocky outcropping that jutted straight up out of the ground.

I looked at my dad to see if he wanted to go up these very

steep rocks. After racing up the sheer rocks, I looked back at my dad, who was struggling to climb up.

I then heard him say, "I knew you would go this way, you crazy cat."

I waited for him and amazingly, he navigated his way up to where I was.

What he had just climbed impressed me, so I gave him a little look telling him let's go higher.

My ability to jump and leap allowed me to race up the face of these very steep rocks with ease.

I was truly enjoying watching my dad try to keep up with me.

These rocks kept going up higher and higher and soon we were hundreds of feet off the valley floor. I could see the blue truck and tent way down below us.

When we got about halfway up this rock pile, the view was intense.

We could see in three directions and there was a layer of clouds rising up from below.

They seemed to dissipate when they reached the elevation that we were at, exposing the grand view of the massive valley that lurked down below.

Way down at the bottom of this valley, you could see the outline of Lake George peering up at us.

Where we were climbing was twenty miles from the lake and at least 2000 feet in elevation higher.

I was very excited and had never experienced such an awesome display of color and magnitude.

With the sun slowly rising above us, this phenomenal and spectacular view was truly enlightening my senses.

Even the smell of the forest was more delightful than usual!

My dad and I were having a great day and after resting a while, we headed up towards the top of this massively steep rock pile.

The rocks at this elevation seem to have a valley up through them that allowed us an easier way to the top. I followed this natural trail and soon afterwards, I spotted a chipmunk scurrying away.

I raced after it, but couldn't catch this fast and elusive varmint. Soon afterwards, I picked up the scent of another chipmunk on top of this rocky outcropping I was walking across. I followed it until I came to a watering hole.

There, I could smell the scent of several different kinds of varmints, including the rabbit.

The rocks had depressions in them in this certain spot.

When it rained, the water must flow down to these small depressions, making a natural watering hole for all the creatures in the area.

I was really thirsty after all the climbing, so I took advantage of this natural phenomenon, and got me a drink!

My dad saw me drinking and commented to me, that I was pretty smart for locating this drinking hole.

After refreshing myself, I noticed that we were not far from the top. I quickly headed that way to see what was up there.

I was absolutely amazed and delighted from the spectacular view that was present at the top of these steep and massive rocks.

I scurried to the highest spot where I could see in every direction.

There, I took a seat to enjoy the grand scenery. Then I noticed that my dad was taking my picture.

He commented to me that I looked like the King of the Mountain!

Then he said he would be right up. I enjoyed watching him struggle to navigate up to where I was.

After making it up to the top through this steep and difficult section, I heard big dad scream in excitement.

He then picked me up and gave me a big hug. He told me how proud he was of me for leading the way to the top.

This was the most fun I have ever had hiking with my big dad!

It was so exhilarating climbing up those steep rocks to get to the top, that I was truly feeling pumped up and ready to explore.

Even though the view was great, I just couldn't sit still. I needed to go check out this steep and massive rock nose that we were resting on.

I immediately went to the south edge of this nose and realized that it was too steep to climb down. There was a 300-foot cliff staring me in the face. I heard my dad say, "Be careful, you crazy cat!" I then ventured around to the west and discovered a steep, but rain-pitted slope that led down to another level.

I quickly managed to navigate down this rock using the rain-pitted holes for traction.

Now I was on this huge ledge that had steep drop-offs on all sides. I slowly crept towards the edge of this massive rock structure.

The adrenaline rush was intense, so I bravely headed along the edge to see what was down there.

I saw nothing but danger! There were sharp and jagged rocks laying in wait, down below.

When I turned around, I noticed my dad climbing down towards me, using the same rain-pitted holes for traction.

He is so smart and I like how he tracks me down. After joining back up with me, big dad reached down and patted me on the head, saying, "You are a brave cat!"

I indeed, was feeling brave and very pumped up.

This adventure that we were on was absolutely fantastic and I was having a complete blast!

I then headed towards the north along this ledge, until I came to a large crack in the rock that separated us from continuing on.

This crack in the ledge was about three-and-a-half feet wide and dropped straight down about 200 yards.

With my dad watching, I didn't hesitate one second before I leaped across to the other side.

I then looked back to see if my dad was going to attempt this dangerous jump.

This large crack definitely presented a challenge to my dad, and after thoroughly looking over the problem, I watched him step back several feet.

Then he said to me, "Watch out. I'm coming across!"

Then big dad ran as fast as he could and jumped across safely.

I was impressed with his ability and continued to lead the way around the entire rock nose, with my dad following.

When we reached the top of this rocky ridge, we were very close to the trail that led us up to the top from the east.

I was feeling exhausted, so I found a really comfortable spot to lay, right on top of this smooth and colorful slab of Colorado Rocky Mountain granite!

My dad liked my idea, and took off his boots. He then sat down and took another picture of me enjoying myself on this awesome adventure.

The sun was starting to set, so after I rested up, my dad and I continued to explore this huge rock structure.

We kept heading north along the top until we came to a group of caves. The ledge that we were on was lower in elevation than the very top, and these caves seemed to be formed by the water running down from up above. They were very smooth and were hooked together by thin channels.

These caves were just big enough for me to fit inside, so I slithered in to see where they went.

Inside, I could smell the faint scent of a chipmunk. The rocks inside the cave were incredibly smooth and cool to the touch.

There was light coming in from above, and it was angled from left to right. I followed the brightness through an oval opening that was like a rock funnel, until I reached the top.

The rocks were still very smooth and I enjoyed walking on them. I went to the edge to see where my dad was.

He was standing about eight feet below me and didn't see me standing up there watching him.

I then meowed at him to get his attention, and I think he was surprised because he was expecting me to come out where I went in.

I was over joyed with pleasure out exploring with my big dad! It amazes me that he knows about these really cool spots, and even more so, that he takes me here so I can enjoy it.

My dad is the best!

I was having so much fun, that I didn't realize that we had been out exploring for more than three hours. The sun had already set, and we were still on top of this massive rock pile.

Then my dad picked me up to give me a hug and asked me if I was ready to head back to the camp.

I was very excited, so I decided to take us down a different way. We were heading back to the east, towards the truck, but on a much steeper slope than we had come up on.

I love how my dad lets me lead the way, and even though I was taking him down a dangerous decline, he managed to keep up and never complained.

I could sense that there was an easier way off this rock down below. I just had to get us there!

It was starting to get dark, so I navigated a way that the water must take, to get us down and off this very steep and smooth rock.

There was a very narrow channel that had several three-to-four-foot drop-offs, so I headed that way by slowly jumping down one at a time.

After getting down, I looked back up, to see if my dad was following. Incredibly, he was right there, looking down at me! Then I heard him mumbling about how brave and crazy I was for taking us this way.

I waited for him to climb down this intense, difficult and steep waterfall-like section, with the flashlight and stool securely slung over his right shoulder.

I was impressed at what I just watched my dad accomplish. I didn't think he would be able to get down.

We were now on a rocky ledge that was much flatter and easier to stand on. There were rock walls on both sides, and this crevasse was very narrow.

I headed down about twenty-five feet along this ledge before the left side opened up into a cave that a bear or mountain lion could fit in.

I immediately went in to check it out. This was the biggest cave that I had ever been in.

Inside, I started sniffing around to see if I could smell if anything had been here recently.

Soon after, I noticed my dad shining his flashlight on me.

It was almost dark outside, and my dad and I were still exploring. How cool is that?

He crawled into the cave until he was right next to me and then shined the flashlight all around so we could see clearly.

Unbelievably, as we were sitting there inside this really cool cave, the flashlight started to go dim.

My dad said to me, "We'd better go. My flashlight batteries are almost dead."

Instinctively, I knew that I needed to lead the way, because with no flashlight, my dad would have a hard time seeing in the dark.

There was no moon tonight, and it was almost pitch black outside.

I carefully navigated the rock ledge until I reached the dirt slope that I knew waited for us down below.

Now that we were off the rocks, the walking became much easier.

I went slow, so big dad could see my tail and follow me in the dark.

Then, in a place I had never been to before, in the dark, I led my dad three quarters of a mile through the forest back to the camp.

Chapter Nine
MICE IN THE HOUSE

When we got back to the campsite, I was pumped up and extremely hungry. I was feeling very proud of myself for leading us back through the forest, in the dark!

I could read my dad's mind. He was impressed with my ability to see in the dark and lead us straight back to the truck in an area we did not know! He felt lucky that I was with him to show him the way back.

After big dad unzipped the door to the tent, I ran inside to find dinner. He had smartly set up my feeding bowls on a soft towel folded in layers. As I lay there comfortably eating, I thought about the awesome adventure I just had with my dad, hiking to the top of the spot I named Rock Mountain.

I was so hungry that I ate the entire bowl of crunchy cat snacks. Then I drank up almost all the water in my other bowl.

After dinner, I went outside to hide in the darkness. I was hoping to find me a varmint!

As I hid at a distance, I could see a faint blue glow coming from the tent, created by the LED light that dad had turned on.

I heard him cooking up some dinner as I silently lay there in the pitch black of the night.

I was so happy that I couldn't help softly purring to myself.

Being out in the Colorado forest with my dad truly was making all my dreams come true!

A short while later, I heard my dad say that he was going to bed. I was so exhausted, that I didn't wait for him to call me and quickly joined him.

After jumping up into the back of the Toyota truck, I found the coat with the silk lining and smartly slid in to get comfortable.

I heard dad zip up the tent door before joining me in the back of the truck.

He then leaned over and kissed me on the head before turning out the lights.

As we lay there in the darkness, big dad told me he loved me and that he would take me exploring again tomorrow.

I felt so happy and safe, I fell asleep immediately.

The morning came quickly before I was woken by the sound of a bird chirping. I thought I might be dreaming, but then I heard my dad softly snoring.

I remembered that we were camping and wanted to get up immediately.

I decided to wake up big dad by walking over his head slowly, as I headed toward the exit.

This maneuver woke him up fast, and he said to me, "What are you doing, you crazy cat?"

I meowed back with this double meow that I didn't even know I knew!

My dad is so cool, he got up immediately. After we both got a drink, he grabbed the three-legged stool, the water, and the snacks, then opened up the tent door. I quickly ran outside to learn that the sun hadn't even come up yet.

I accidentally on purpose had gotten us up really early so we could explore everything!

Then, as we walked away from the campsite with me leading

and big dad following, I heard him say to me, "Where did you learn that cool sounding double meow that you woke me up with?"

I looked back at him and repeated that double meow I had just learned. It did sound kinda cool, and I was delighted that he had noticed my accidental meowing flaw, caused by overwhelming excitement!

As we headed off into the forest in a different direction, I started thinking about how cool my dad is for not being mad at me for walking over his head this morning. This was the first time I had used this head-walking maneuver to wake him up, and unbelievably, it worked perfectly!

My goal today was to explore the entire forest south of the rock mountain and west of the campsite.

After traveling into the forest and across a grassy meadow, we came to a pile of flattened rocks that seemed to be the high spot between the meadows and just south of Rock Mountain.

There, I spotted the first chipmunk of the day, running the other way. I quickly raced after it and trapped it under a medium-sized boulder.

I ran around this rock, hoping the chipmunk would want to come out and play. It never did!

My dad finally caught up and commented to me that I looked cool chasing after this chipmunk through these colorful rocks.

These rocks did look radical! They were completely weathered smooth, colored red, and had colorful moss growing on all sides except the south-facing one.

I climbed to the highest spot to get a good view. There, I could see that I was on the same rocks as yesterday, but just much lower and to the south.

I could see east and west over two identical meadows, and to the south was an aspen grove.

I looked at my dad and hoped he could read my mind that I wanted to head back up to the top of Rock Mountain on this south-facing slope!

This way was steep and treacherous, and after I raced up a couple hundred yards, I looked back to see if my dad was following.

He was struggling, but amazingly followed me up. At times we were out of view of each other because I would be higher, exploring new openings or caves while I waited for him.

I could smell the scent of chipmunks and rabbits everywhere.

I felt like an experienced rock climber as I raced higher and higher.

I felt so strong that climbing up these steep rocks didn't scare me.

Every time I would get higher up, I looked back to see if my crazy dad was still following.

He truly does amaze me that he can navigate his way up these rocks and keep up with me.

Soon, I came to the bottom of the 300-foot cliff that I stood on top of yesterday. There, I looked around for anything to move while I waited for my dad to catch up.

After big dad climbed up this steep incline to where I was resting, he picked me up to give me a hug.

Then, while he was holding me, he said to me, "Lucky-Son-Jones, you really are a crazy, brave cat." Then he said, "I never thought you would be such a good rock climber."

I was tickled that he thought so highly of me, and even more so that he was spending time with me so I could learn.

What a great dad I have!

Then, big dad said, "What are you going to do now? We certainly can't climb up this cliff face."

While I was waiting for him, I discovered a steep but doable path around this cliff to the west.

To the east was too steep to climb up. Then I gave him a look, and a little meow to follow me!

I headed up this steep rain-pitted rocky slope that led me to a cave. I reached this opening quickly, but noticed big dad was hesitating to follow me!

I heard him say, "It is to steep for me, I'm heading across and around."

I then went into this cave to explore and saw light coming in from the other side.

This cave went in about forty feet, right through an incredibly straight up and down rock outcropping.

There were a lot of small jagged rocks lining the floor of this cave, which made it difficult to cross.

On the other side of this cave, as I was looking downwards, I could hear the breathing sound of my dad, who had gone down and around to keep up with his little buddy!

I soon saw him coming around this steep rock outcropping, way down below.

When we made eye contact, I was glad that he had figured out a way to keep up.

I was so excited that we were rock climbing together, I just couldn't stand still.

I slowly started navigating towards the north along this ridge that was steep and cliff-like. Big dad was about thirty yards down below traversing up at an angle towards me. There were a lot of fallen boulders that we had to climb on or around.

I was starting to wonder if the way I had taken us was going to lead us to the top or not. It was really steep.

Dad finally caught up with me, and then we both took a little break together. After snacking and getting a drink, I headed off to find us a way to the top of Rock Mountain from the west side.

Amazingly, after traveling another 200 yards, I came to this ravine in the cliff-like slope that we were on.

This crack was about three feet wide, and even though the surface was steep, it was relatively flat and easy to climb for both of us.

I led the way, and big dad followed. This crack in the rock gave us an easy way up a very steep and rocky slope.

We soon reached the top and both dad and I were elated that we had found this unbelievably easy way up.

We were now in the middle of Rock Mountain, at its highest

point. Yesterday we were more south, at Rock Mountain's highest peak.

What a blast I was having hiking and rock climbing with my dad!

We spent most of the day exploring around the top of Rock Mountain.

First, I led us to the north, scurrying across the flat and smooth rocks of the summit. Within minutes I saw a female mule deer with her fawn down below us, just fifty yards away.

They were hiding in a small grassy meadow in the shade of these really cool-looking thin and narrow-shaped pine trees.

I stopped and thought to myself, "How did these deer get up here to the top of Rock Mountain? All the paths to the summit were steep and technical."

For the rest of the day as I hunted, I searched for the way these deer would have taken to get up here.

I slowly prowled around these hiding mule deer, and within twenty minutes, I located the first chipmunk of the day.

It saw me coming and ran along the smooth rocks at an incredible speed. It made it to a thin crack in the rocks where they protruded up, to hide.

Today, big dad was making it easy for me to hunt. Instead of being noisy when he walked, the flat and smooth rocks of the summit kept him quiet and stealth-like.

I immediately sat outside the opening that the chipmunk had disappeared into. Within seconds, big dad asked me if I needed some help. I meowed back, "I sure do!"

Then, he smartly knelt down on top of this flat rock, directly over the horizontal crack that the chipmunk was hiding in.

I got myself completely ready! I was crouched down and dug into the surface of the rock with my claws, anticipating that my dad might scare it my way.

Dad was about three feet away and two feet higher than me on the rock.

The horizontal crack in this elevated rock only opened up to the north and was about five feet long.

It went in about ten inches and was just big enough to hide a frightened chipmunk. Then big dad worked his magic! He leaned over while on his hands and knees and blew loudly into the crack.

Sure enough, the chipmunk thought that the blowing noise was me, and was scared into running the other way. It ran out of the horizontal crack in a fury, not seeing me hiding in ambush down below!

I sprang forward and caught this supercharged varmint. The rocks were too hard to play on, so I took the chipmunk to a nearby grassy field.

There, I dropped it out of my mouth, hoping it would run. This varmint lay on the ground for a few seconds while it looked up at me.

Then, it decided it wanted to play, and jumped up to run. This chipmunk was definitely faster than any I had caught before. It took all my strength and speed to catch and subdue it the first few times.

Eventually, it started to slow down in exhaustion. This was a very fast chipmunk who used a different technique to escape than all the others.

Instead of biting and clawing to escape, which usually triggers my instinct to kill, it laid there on its back and stared at me!

Then, I would look away, trying to fool it into thinking I wasn't watching. This trick worked perfectly, and it would jump up and run away so I could chase after and retrieve it.

After playing together for about twenty minutes, I decided to let this chipmunk go by letting it escape up a tree.

This supercharged chipmunk never once bit me or tried to claw at my eyes. I had fun playing, so I decided not to hurt it and let it go.

My dad was standing close by and said to me, "It still counts, even though it got away."

He thought that the chipmunk had managed to escape, rather than I let it go. Silly dad!

Big dad then told me the bad news that it was time to go and pack up the camp.

I was saddened, but knew this moment was coming!

Instinctively, I led the way, heading east down a different way than the first time. We were still located toward the center of Rock Mountain as we traveled down. When the rocks ran out and it turned to dirt and grass, I figured out how those two mule deer had managed to get all the way up to the top.

There was a natural grass ravine that hid itself on the east face, in between all the rock outcroppings. It was steep and went down several hundred yards before turning into the forest. There, the slope was not as intense and gradually fanned out to flatter ground.

We were now down off of Rock Mountain and traveling through the forest that was getting thicker with every step. This part of the forest was very dense and lush-looking. I slowly navigated my way towards the camp.

A little while later, I could see the blue Toyota truck and tent coming into view up ahead.

After we returned to the campsite, it didn't take dad long to dismantle and pack up all of the camping supplies. I was hiding in a nearby meadow, trying to find a mouse, when I heard him call for me.

It did not take us long to return home. After jumping out of the truck, I took my time heading to the house.

Soon after dad opened up the front door, I heard him call my name. When I went inside, he told me that he had just seen two mice running through the kitchen and that he wanted me to catch them A.S.A.P!

I ran into the kitchen and could hear their squeaks behind the stove. As they hid in fear, I decided to relax and get a bite to eat.

That night, after following my dad into the bedroom, I laid at the corner of the bed with one eye open. As I tried to fall asleep, I just couldn't figure out how two mice had gotten into the house.

I remember bringing in only one mouse, that I let go!

About two hours after I fell asleep, I was woken up by some scratching sounds. I quietly jumped down from the bed and slowly prowled into the living room, where the sounds were emanating from. I tiptoed down the back edge of the sofa and took a spot at its corner. There, I could see into the kitchen and dining area.

As I sat there listening, I saw something move on the carpet below the dining table.

I got myself ready by digging my claws into the carpet and lifted my hind quarters for the attack!

Then, I was stopped dead in my tracks by seeing not one or two, but three small mice running into the kitchen right in front of me.

As I watch them run onto the wooden floor towards my feeding bowls, I thought to myself, "Where did all these mice come from?"

I held my position to stay hidden, so I could see what these mice were up to.

These little varmints were stealing my food and hiding it everywhere. Under the stove, in the food pantry and other spots in the dining room.

I had seen enough and decided to take action! Without hesitation, I sprinted forward towards two of these mice that were heading towards the dining area with my food.

It was too late for these young mice because I was already sliding across the carpet on my side with lightning speed.

Just like when I am playing mouse in the house with my dad, with the fake mouse on the string.

As these mice ran from the wooden floor of the kitchen onto the rug of the dining area, I was there and caught them both red-handed.

With precision sliding and accurate reaching, I nabbed up both mice, one in one paw and one in the other!

I was now feasting on mice, right here in the dining area. How's that for intelligent hunting? I knew my dad would be proud of me, so I left him a couple of mouse tails and hindquarters on the carpet at the kill spot, so he would know I was up all night hunting.

After taking my place back at the corner of the couch, I thought about the mouse that I had caught in the winter time, and then let go in the house.

This mouse must have been pregnant and gave birth somewhere in the house, right under my unsuspecting nose.

I kept on the prowl for a mouse in the house every night for the next two weeks. Eventually, I caught and killed the entire mouse family hiding in the house.

All this tasty protein is making my fur very soft and shiny, and I truly enjoy the benefits of hunting inside the house!

Chapter Ten
DR. LEMMONS

The next day after our morning walk in paradise, I saw my dad open up the cardboard box that he had brought me home in when he adopted me.

This box had a handle on top with tiny air holes drilled in all around. It was just big enough for a cat to fit into and when I saw him open it, I thought to myself. "I wonder what he is doing?"

Then, all of a sudden I was swept up and placed into this open box.

When he started closing up the top I was thinking, "Pretty funny, now let me out!"

My dad started talking to me and said that he was taking me to the veterinarian for a checkup and to get my yearly shots.

I was now feeling a little bit nervous being inside this box. The last time I was placed into this box I was in kitty jail.

I wasn't sure what going to the veterinarian meant. Was he taking me back to jail?

I immediately started to read his mind, to find out what was going on.

I was so relieved when I discovered that he was taking me to a new veterinarian named Doctor Lemons for my rabies and distemper shots.

I remember getting these shots about a year ago, and the good memory of the doctor in the white coat with a funny long thing wrapped around her neck.

I was now kind of excited to go visit with this new doctor.

My dad carried me out to the truck in this stylish cardboard travel box.

I wasn't afraid this time when I was placed into the Toyota truck. After we started moving down the driveway, big dad opened up the box so I could see out.

I was facing him as I laid there in this box. I looked up at him and thought to myself, "What a cool dad I have for taking me to see the doctor."

After a few minutes went by, I climbed out of the box and took my usual spot on my dad's lap. He rolled down the window so I could stick my head out to get some fresh air.

When we arrive at the veterinarian's office I was placed back inside the travel box.

Then, he carried me inside and place me on the floor right next to a big dog in a cage!

I heard him talking to the receptionist while he filled out some paperwork. I could barely see out of the tiny air holes in this box I was trapped in. Over in the corner of the room, I could see another big dog on a leash, breathing hard.

I felt kind of frightened by these dogs before we were quickly led into one of the examining rooms down the hall.

My dad opened up the box and I jumped out immediately to start exploring.

There were lots of animal smells all around this room and I soon located the scent of a female cat.

I sniffed intensely trying to soak up her smell. Then, I laid down and rolled my head in her aroma.

A few minutes later the doctor's aide came into the room to get some information on me.

After writing some stuff down on her tablet, she commented to my dad that I was so beautiful and very well-behaved.

I looked at her and thought to myself, "Well, of course, I am good. I am a "Royal Psychic Super Cat!"

My dad was stunned that I didn't run and hide in fear when the aide entered the room.

He knows that I am afraid of most strangers and that I usually flee, to disappear and hide.

I was feeling very excited while we waited for the new doctor to come in. It wasn't long before a lady in a white coat came into the room wearing that funny long-looking thing around her neck.

She was an older lady who talked softly and seemed really nice.

After my dad placed me on the table, I walked around strutting my stuff to show the doctor how big I was.

She told dad to hold onto me while she looked into my ears. The doctor said that my ears were a little bit dirty, but could be easily cleaned if done carefully.

She also looked at my teeth and eyes, while commenting that I was a beautiful cat!

She said that my teeth were very white and healthy-looking and that my fur was absolutely gorgeous.

I felt proud because I do spend a lot of time grooming and cleaning myself.

Then, she listened to my heartbeat for a while with that funny-looking device around her neck before she said, "We are almost done!"

Her soft voice and tender touch tickled my senses. As the doctor wrote into her charts, she told my dad that I was a very well-behaved young cat!

Then, Dr. Lemons pulled on my fur near my thigh and before I knew it, she was done giving me both of my shots.

Her technique was fast and painless!

I looked over at my dad to read his mind. He was thinking, "For a cat who is afraid of strangers, you sure are eating this attention up. What a crazy cat!"

On the way home, I laid on my dad's lap and purred in appreciation for what he had just done. These shots will keep me safe this summer if I catch a sick varmint. What a great dad I have. I truly love him.

Shortly after we got home, I heard my dad call my name.

I went into the living room where he was waiting for me. He had a bowl of warm water and some Q-tips close by.

Then, I was swiftly picked up and placed between my dad's thighs while he knelt down on the carpet. He held me in place with his legs by gently squeezing them together.

I immediately read his mind to find out what he was doing.

Dr. Lemons had told him my ears were dirty, so he decided that he would try and gently clean them for me.

He first started with the right ear by softly grasping it with his left hand. He held it in between his thumb and forefinger at the tip so he could gently pull open my ear to see inside.

Then he said, " Holy cow, your ear *is* dirty!" He talked to me as he gently held my ear open with his left hand while smartly covering my eyes with his fingers.

This maneuver kept me from seeing what was going on, so I wouldn't be frightened.

I trusted my dad as he methodically cleaned the inside of my right ear. He changed the Q-tips often because they got dirty quickly.

His gentle strokes felt incredibly good as he pulled this dirty, waxy substance out of my ear.

After getting my ear cleaned, big dad then rubbed the fur on the outside of my ear with his thumb and forefinger.

Then, he repeated the exact same process with my left ear. I never thought that the inside of my ears could be cleaned, and now that they have, I can honestly say I feel better, and my hearing has improved.

My Dad's quick ear-cleaning session was painless and I truly enjoyed every minute.

Afterwards, he lightly scratched the fur on top of my head in between my ears. He then kissed me on top of the head while he released me from his grasp.

Big dad is a gentle giant and I won't mind getting my ears cleaned again.

I ran over to my cardboard cat scratcher, to tear it up! After sharpening my claws, I was feeling kind of sassy, so I laid down on my scratcher and ate some of the catnip that my dad had given me.

Then, for some reason, I felt the need to roll my head and ears in the rest of this catnip. After doing this, I now had catnip stuck in my fur all around my head and freshly cleaned ears.

I was feeling so relaxed and comfortable sprawled out on the wooden floor of the kitchen that I fell asleep soon afterward.

Chapter Eleven
NO DIESEL TRUCKS

This morning I had to wake up my dad twice because he did not want to get up early. It was still dark outside and I felt like going hunting.

First, I jumped up onto the bed and walked right across big dad's head in an attempt to wake him.

Then, after I did this a second time my dad woke up and said to me, "What are you doing you crazy cat?"

I started meowing at him to get up. I was ready to go outside to do some early-morning prowling.

He wasn't responding and getting up like he usually does, so I kept on meowing at him.

After about 25 meows, my dad threw a pillow in my direction and told me to shut up!

I kept meowing, hoping he would get up. Then, my dad did something that surprised me! He started meowing back at me.

Every time I meowed, he would meow twice. I meowed faster, hoping he would get the message and get up!

Then, he meowed faster and louder in an attempt to antagonize me into shutting up.

I was feeling a little anxious this morning, but I soon realized that big dad was probably as annoyed as I was about all the meowing going on!

He quickly got his point across to me, that there is no need for all that meowing noise this early in the morning!

From that day forward, I never irritated my dad again with the multiple meowing session.

Amazingly, big dad is really good about getting up early and taking me outside, just not this morning!

Finally, after slowly getting up, my dad grabbed the supplies we needed for our morning walk.

With the three-legged stool slung over his shoulder, he opened up the front door so we could go outside.

The air smelled good but there was a constant noise coming from the neighbor's house that is usually vacant.

For the last couple of weeks, there has been a loud and irritating noise coming from our neighbor's generator, day and night.

I looked up at my dad and could read his mind, that he too is annoyed by this new and constant sound.

Apparently, our ignorant neighbor has decided to invade our peace and quiet time by letting his new renters run the propane generator instead of fixing his solar system for the house.

Even out in the middle of Colorado, deep in the forest where there are few people living, there are still idiots who want to invade our privacy.

Twenty acres of land is supposed to protect against this kind of intrusion!

Today, I decided to head away from this noise toward our other neighbor's house at a very quick pace.

This neighbor's name is John, and he lives in the opposite direction away from all this noise pollution. My dad and he are friends.

I hurried to get us away from this generator sound that was buzzing my ears.

Big dad yelled at me to slow down and take it easy on him.

I didn't realize it, but I was so excited about getting us away from the noise that I was almost running at a full trot!

Once I got us over the ridge between John's house and our property, the noise became less and less.

My poor dad was grunting and moaning in pain, trying to keep up with my super fast pace.

When the noise wasn't as loud, I slowed down to let big dad catch up. I soon realized that I had taken us completely past John's property, and further south than we had ever been.

This was all new territory for me to explore, so I led the way and big dad followed. Straight ahead, I could see a dirt road that I had never seen before. I could hear the sound of water trickling, so I headed that way.

After reading my dad's mind, I learned that the dirt road that we had just come to, was the main dirt road that led to our dirt road.

We started walking down this road until we came to a natural spring that overflowed into a three-foot-deep, round steel tub.

I immediately headed towards the sound of this trickling water, hoping I would find me an unsuspecting varmint drinking close by.

When I got near the steel pond, I could see water flowing over the east side of it and down a shallow rocky drainage ditch that headed back towards the road.

The sound of this crystal clear Rocky Mountain spring water flowing, enticed me into getting a drink!

I wasn't able to drink for very long because the water was extremely cold and made my tongue numb.

After getting a drink, I followed the water down the left side of this new dirt road that we had just found.

Within seconds, I saw a rabbit darting away towards the east. I headed that way and soon picked up the scent of this fleeing rabbit.

I tracked this rabbit through some shrub oak bushes and into a grassy meadow that headed downwards, towards a steep rocky ridge.

At the edge of this meadow, I could hear the rabbit hopping through the grass at a fast pace trying to escape, and soon located it down below.

It was now too far away from me to have a good chance at catching it!

I looked back to see if big dad was following. I could hear him coming, so I headed towards the steep rocky ridge that loomed in front of us.

We had never been this way before, so I was having a blast exploring this new terrain.

The best part of our morning adventure was that we were now far enough away from that generator noise! The buzzing in my ears had subsided, and once again I could hear really good.

Big dad was keeping up as we headed towards these steep rocks. I couldn't wait to start climbing and searching.

I instinctively knew there would be some kind of varmint hiding, so I slowed down my approach to give myself a better chance of hearing or seeing something move.

I snuck up beside a small gray boulder that was the same size as me. There, I held my position trying to stay camouflaged. As I looked around I realized that I had entered the shady zone of the rocky ridge.

I was completely camouflaged, and if it wasn't for the noise that my dad was making as he walked towards me, I think I could have caught me a chipmunk.

There was a whole family of them running about just above me, but when they heard my dad coming they started running away and screaming out their alert sounds to warn the others of the danger.

I was sure that they hadn't seen me, so I was disappointed at the missed opportunity.

I quickly moved and headed towards the rocks. I was feeling strong and pumped up, so I jumped up about five and a half feet onto one rock and then another four feet onto another rock that had a flat top. Within seconds I was high above my dad and his noisy boots. I looked back to see if he would follow me this way or try another. He headed towards the right, to navigate the steep slope up between the boulders.

I headed straight, leaping up and over many boulders until I reached the top.

Immediately, I saw a chipmunk so I went racing after it. Soon afterward, this frightened chipmunk found security under a five-foot diameter Colorado mountain boulder.

I sniffed intensely as I prowled around the entire boulder. I could hear and smell it hiding under there, so I quickly jumped up five feet to be on top of this rock for the attack!

Then, I heard my dad calling for me. He was at the top of the ridge looking for me. Somehow, I had managed to get myself several hundred feet below the top of this ridge racing after this chipmunk.

As I stood on top of this five-foot boulder, I meowed towards my dad so he would know where I was.

After he found me, he couldn't believe that I was crouched down on top of this huge boulder, hunting a noisy chipmunk.

Then, I heard him say, "You are a big, crazy cat!"

I read my dad's mind and he was thinking, "I would have never found you if you hadn't meowed back to me when I called."

Then, big dad asked me if I needed some help. I stood up, and because I was as tall as he was, I looked him straight in the eyes and meowed back, "I sure do!"

I quickly jumped down and took a spot close to one of the openings under this rock. Big dad went around to the other side and asked me if I was ready.

I meowed back, "Yes!" Then I heard him loudly blow into a hole under this large Colorado boulder.

After a couple of loud blows, this noisy chipmunk came darting out and ran up a nearby tree. Unfortunately, I can't catch them all!

I love hunting with my dad. After getting a hug, I headed back up this ridge towards the south. The sun had risen high in the eastern sky as we reached the top of this ridge. The view looking south was beautiful and the wind was breezy.

I just love being outside spending time with my dad.

After looking around awhile, I started leading us back the way we came. Over the hill and through the woods, back to the house we went.

I saw a few more varmints on the way home, but today I didn't catch anything. It was very peaceful traveling home because the neighbor had turned off their generator.

We were close to home when my greatest fear of all happened! The sound of a diesel truck, close by.

I was located slightly downhill and about thirty feet from the dirt road that led to our driveway. Then all of a sudden, this diesel truck came racing around a bend in the road and right by me.

The thundering sound of that diesel truck flying by absolutely scared me to death!

All I could think about was that man in the diesel truck must have seen me and was coming to get me and take me back to kitty jail!

There is no way I was going to let that happen ever again!

Even with my dad watching out for me, I was not going to give anyone in a diesel truck a chance to catch me.

I immediately raced off at full throttle in the opposite direction, until I disappeared into the forest.

I heard my dad calling for me, but I just ignored him. I am not going back to jail!

I ran until I was sure that nobody could catch me. I was now close to the boulder pile near our house, so I went and hid among these precious rocks.

I was so scared that I was shaking!

After finding a good hiding spot with a view, I started to relax, knowing that I could flee higher into the rocks if I saw anyone coming.

I knew this boulder pile like the back of my paw, and gradually I started to feel safe.

A short while later I fell asleep with one eye open in this comfortable spot, completely camouflaged by the shade of this large gray boulder.

I didn't nap for very long and I slept lightly to make sure nobody could sneak up on me. I was woken up by the heat of the afternoon sun. With the sun setting in the west, I was no longer in the shade, so I quickly decided to relocate.

After stretching out, I started to head to the top of the boulder pile to check out the view and to see if there were any varmints running around.

Being by myself today, I am hoping that I will have better luck hunting. The rocks in and around the boulder pile are gray and very smooth. It is easy for me to approach quietly and stay camouflaged with my grey and black tiger striping.

After sneaking through a five-inch opening between these two massive boulders, I saw my first chipmunk of the day laying on the rocks, sunning itself.

I was almost at the top, which gave me a great view of the entire ridge. My stealth-like movements allowed me to approach this chipmunk undetected, and slowly I got myself to about three feet away.

I crouched down as low as I could get, hoping I would surprise this napping varmint.

Being just west of this chipmunk and with the sun setting, I knew from experience that the sun's rays would blind the chipmunk if it looked in my direction.

I took a couple of deep breaths and prepared to attack!

I had smartly gotten myself in the perfect location and was salivating over the taste of a yummy chipmunk for dinner.

Then, with perfect cunning and precision leaping, I landed right on top of this unsuspecting sleeping varmint.

I immediately took it to the very top where I knew there was a small play area. This chipmunk was not happy about being captured, and when I released it from my grasp it surprisingly attacked.

After charging at me and biting my lip, I became completely enraged.

I then retaliated with a full force cat attack, clamping down on this varmint's neck and throat.

After dining, I remembered that I was missing in action!

I knew my dad must be worried about me, but I was still too frightened to risk heading home.

The sun was setting, so I jumped up to the top of the highest boulder to watch the sunset.

There were a few clouds on the horizon, and as the sun disappeared they all turned a mighty orange color.

Then as the daylight faded, these same clouds changed to a misty reddish-black color. Absolutely beautiful!

While it was getting dark, I contemplated on which one of the neighbors' houses I was going to secretly explore.

I was feeling brave being a large Colorado mountain cat, and seeing how I was already outside, I decided that I would risk being out for the night so I could explore the entire neighborhood!

With no moon tonight, I was excited about being camouflaged by the darkness and sneaking around undetected.

I had never been to a couple of our neighbors' houses on our road, so I put them first on my to-do list for the night.

Chapter Twelve
FIRST OF NINE LIVES

I was just about to head down out of the boulder pile to explore when I heard my dad calling my name.

I immediately held my position, because I did not want to go home yet.

My dad was smartly looking for me at the base of the boulder pile, but he did not come up. It was almost dark now, and I could hear his fading footsteps as he headed down the dirt road. He kept calling for me several times as he headed toward the house.

Now that I'm older, I felt the need to experience being outside all night. I was disobedient and did not listen to my dad when he called.

I remembered the nights that I spent out in the forest of Buena Vista when I was younger, so I couldn't wait to go hunting in the darkness. Without that stupid bell around my neck and all my newly learned hunting experience, I just knew I was going to have better luck hunting.

When I couldn't hear my dad anymore, I slowly headed towards the house of the lady with all the cats. Her name is Katrina.

Along the way, I smartly stopped periodically to look and listen for danger. I knew I needed to be careful to ensure my safety. After arriving at our neighbor's house, I headed directly towards her large cat cage located under the back porch.

Her cats had been outside recently because their scents were strong. I sniffed around intensely to take in all their smells. Even though I had been neutered, I was still very interested in the smell of female cats.

I had all night, so I took my time exploring around this large cage. I could smell four different female cats and one male.

Then I jumped up onto the back porch to see what I could find.

Immediately, I heard this low snarling hiss of a cat. One of her cats was sitting in an open window behind the screen, not too happy about me being out there free to roam around!

I knew I wasn't welcome, so I headed off toward the neighbor that I've never been to before. They live in the first house on our dirt road.

The sign on the driveway said 'Kelly's', so I prowled in close to learn more about them. After sneaking up onto their huge front porch, I could smell a dog!

These people lived in a large log home with a front porch that was decorated with deer antlers and bird feeders.

There were lights on inside but no sign of the people or the dog. I prowled around the entire house searching for a tasty varmint.

It was exhilarating being out in the darkness, and I couldn't wait to find something to catch.

I was impressed with my ability to see in the pitch black of the night and it was so quiet I could hear mice moving around under the front porch, even though I was still out back.

I slowly prowled that way and when I got to the driveway by the porch, I crouched down and silently waited.

Amazingly, I heard a mouse coming my way, so I got myself ready and prepared to attack! Then, all of a sudden I heard a car coming down the dirt road and within seconds, I was being blinded by headlights!

The Kellys were coming home late and had caught me hunting, right in their driveway.

I could barely see as I ran to hide in the forest. After I regained my vision and the adrenaline rush subsided, I decided to head towards our neighbor John's house. He lived directly across the road from us.

I estimated that it was close to midnight, so I carefully prowled through the forest parallel to the dirt road.

It wasn't long before I navigated my way through the darkness to John's property. His driveway was curved and started several hundred feet further down the road than ours.

I had been near John's property many times, but big dad has never let me venture on to it. Anytime I got near or was heading toward his property, big dad always called for me to come.

I read his mind on several occasions to find out why I wasn't permitted to go there.

We all live on 20-acre parcels, and John had a fence around his with no trespassing signs put up.

Big dad always respected this and that's why I wasn't allowed to hunt or go onto John's property.

Well, tonight I was going to be disobedient and check out his entire piece of unexplored territory.

Silently and slowly, I headed towards John's place. His house was located on the other side of a grassy knoll and built up on top of a unique pile of jagged rocks.

I was excited because I could smell varmints close by. As I approach the rocks at the base of John's house, I saw a mouse moving quickly away from me.

I immediately became airborne and leaped on top of this frightened mouse.

After my snack, I searched through all the abundant rocks scattered around John's foundation. There were lots of interesting smells and I found several good hiding spots that the varmints could escape to.

When I got around to the back of his house I noticed an observatory, built smartly on top of a huge boulder with a flat top.

It was easy to get near the structure because the entire boulder was smooth and the north side, closest to John's house, was only elevated a few feet.

After prowling around the observatory, I headed toward the south side of this huge smooth boulder.

I intensely searched for anything that moved.

I was truly disappointed that after all the territory I had already explored, I hadn't seen more varmints to chase or catch.

When I reached the south side of this huge boulder, I came to a cliff that had a twenty-five-foot drop off! There was no way to go any further, so I headed west to get down off this rock.

When I got to the western edge, I jumped down five feet. I was now staring at a large meadow just west of John's observatory.

Out in the middle of this field, there was a cluster of small pine trees. I could barely make out their silhouette as I headed that way.

I prowled slowly, hoping to hear something move and to protect myself from danger.

After reaching the cluster of pine trees, I felt safe so I hung out for a while to see what was going on in the forest this late at night! There was another long and narrow meadow west of where I was hiding, that ran parallel to the road we lived on. This dirt road dead-ended at our other neighbor's house.

My dad and I have never met these people because they only live here a few months in the summertime.

These neighbors were next on my list of things to do tonight.

The quiet of the night was intense as I sat silently hidden among these pine trees.

It was so dark and peaceful. I could hear everything, but I barely could see anything!

Then I heard something move out in the middle of this waiting meadow. I was just about ready to go investigate when I heard a familiar sound.

It was the swooping sound of a large bird whispering through the nighttime air. I knew this sound, and it meant danger!

I held my position and within seconds, I heard the piercing cries of a rabbit. Then, these horrible sounds were lifted up high above me and quickly faded.

Apparently, this rabbit had just been caught by the neighborhood owl and swept away like the wind.

I started to think about how lucky I was for not entering that meadow. Stopping often to protect myself really paid off this time. If I had foolishly crossed into that meadow, I could have been this big owl's next meal!

After the scare, I decided not to go down to the other neighbor's house to explore.

I quickly crossed the road and slowly navigated my way back towards our house, using the edge of the forest for protection.

I had about 400 yards to go to make it to our cabin located at the top of our driveway. I went slowly and stopped at every tree to protect myself in case there was another hungry owl, hiding in the treetops.

When I got to the cabin, I immediately jumped over the four-foot fence and took refuge on the porch.

I knew I would be safe here with a fence surrounding me and a roof overhead. I found a comfortable spot by the wall next to the kindling box.

From this location, I could see down our driveway to the front door of our house. I held my position while I silently hunted until I saw the light of day coming up in the eastern sky.

As I sat there, I thought about my night out in the forest. I came to realize the reason I had not seen many varmints throughout the night was probably because it was so quiet that they could hear me prowling, even though I did it slowly.

I definitely have better luck hunting in the morning and evening hours with my big dad.

I started thinking about my dad and how he must be worried sick about me.

Then as if he read my mind, big dad opened up the front door and called my name. I was so glad to see him and hear his voice that I sprang up immediately, and ran towards the front door.

When I came into view and my dad saw me, I could sense that he was happy to see me. I could hear it in his voice that he was glad I was all right.

When I reached his feet, he quickly picked me up and gave me this huge loving hug. Then, he said to me, "I am so glad you're not hurt. I was worried about you all night!"

I started to read his mind and he was thinking that I just gave up one of my nine lives, being outside all night in the wilderness of Colorado.

I was amazed that he wasn't mad at me and even more so, how he knew that I had run away in fear of the sound of that diesel truck!

Then, big dad asked me if I was hungry and let me inside for my morning feeding. I love my dad and how he treats me.

Chapter Thirteen
THE VANISHING ACT

Today after our morning walk in the forest, my dad gave me a special gravy snack for being so good!

I love living in paradise and all that it offers.

After giving me a snack, big dad always does something really cool that I like, which no one else has ever done.

While I am eating, he will rub my belly with one hand and gently squeeze my lower back with the other.

He will do this for about thirty seconds while telling me that he can feel that my stomach is hungry. Crazy dad!

He has been doing the special belly rub maneuver from the very first day he brought me home, till now! This feels incredibly good, and the first few times he did this it totally relaxed my nervous belly, so I could eat.

After breakfast, my dad picked me up to give me a big hug. I love how he holds me in his arms while rubbing my neck.

As he is doing this I like to push away from his chest with my front paws to increase the rubbing pressure. When big dad feels me pushing away, he does something really unique. He will hold me so that my body is horizontal to the ground and perpendicular to his chest.

This maneuver puts all of my body weight onto his rubbing hand which creates maximum rubbing pressure on my itchy neck.

Boy does that feel amazing!

I trust my dad and know he will not drop me. This unique method of using gravity to help increase my neck's rubbing pressure is pretty smart! What a great dad I have.

After he put me down, my dad told me that he has to go to the grocery store to get us some food. I meowed back, reminding him how much I love those gravy snacks in a can.

I followed him out into the garage, and while he was cleaning the garbage out of his truck, I searched around for a mouse snack.

Then, when he wasn't looking I jumped up onto the floorboard of the truck and then up onto the seat.

Today I decided that I was going to go for a ride in dad's freshly-cleaned truck.

A few minutes had passed before I heard my dad calling for me. He was getting ready to leave and wanted to locate where I was. I saw him looking for me, so I gave out a little meow!

Big dad couldn't believe that I was waiting for him in the Toyota truck. Then he asked me if I wanted to go for a ride.

As he sat down in the driver's seat, I rubbed up against him in approval. I read his mind and he was happily surprised that I wanted to go with him today.

In the past, I have been a little hesitant about going anywhere in big dad's truck.

I trusted him now and really wanted to know where he goes when he drives away.

I was really excited as we drove up our dirt driveway. I took my usual spot on dad's lap as he rolled down the driver side window.

I was happy traveling in the Toyota, and after we drove a while we entered a large parking lot and came to a stop.

I sat up and looked around. All I could see where buildings, people, and cars. The noise that these vehicles and people were making scared me, so I headed down to the floorboard on the passenger side to hide.

My dad told me not to worry and that he would be back shortly. After he closed the truck door, I jumped up onto the seat to see where he was going.

He was heading towards a large building that said Walmart on the front. After he disappeared, I headed back down to the floorboard of big dad's truck.

A short while later, I heard loud screams and the rumbling sound of a shopping cart close by. The family who parked next to us had returned. The kids were making a lot of noise and horsing around the truck.

Then I felt the truck move after one of the kids bumped into the driver's side mirror.

I started to shake in fear and looked for a better place to hide.

I realized that I was still frightened by strangers when I felt the truck move a second time. Someone in this noisy family had opened their door and dinged the side of my dad's truck.

Now I was really scared, so I desperately looked for a place to hide. There was a small opening about four inches wide and three inches tall, directly under the truck's seat.

Then I heard doors slamming, shopping carts moving, and kids screaming!

I had heard enough frightening noise and needed to hide because of the fear.

From the driver's side floorboard, I dove towards the opening under the seat. I had to wiggle, scratch, and pull, to squeeze through this opening that was barely big enough for me to fit!

Once I got through, I was concealed by a larger area under the truck's seat. I felt safer there but soon realized that I was trapped under the seat because there was no way that I was going back through this tight opening.

I was safe, so I relaxed and got myself comfortable while I waited for my dad's return.

A short while later, I heard the familiar sounds of keys and then the driver's side door opened.

I could see outside through another small opening, and there was big dad standing motionless.

I quickly read his mind, and he was absolutely stunned that I wasn't in the truck. I felt his jaw drop as he frantically looked around while calling out my name.

He knew that someone couldn't have stolen me because the truck was locked and the only thing missing was me!

I was still reading his mind, and after a couple minutes had passed this unbelievably sad and empty feeling overcame my dad's thoughts.

He just couldn't believe that I had vanished into thin air!

Then he looked around outside the truck while calling my name. He knew that I couldn't have jumped out the windows because they were only rolled down one inch.

When he came back around to the driver's side door he was confused, heartbroken, and extremely upset. I could really feel how much he loves me and didn't want him to worry anymore, so I let out a little meow!

At first, he thought he was hearing things, but after I meowed again he saw me hiding there under the truck's seat.

I could hear the joy in his voice as he said, "You crazy cat. How did you get yourself under there?"

He knew that the openings under the truck's seat were small and just couldn't believe that I had managed to get through one of them.

Then big dad said, "Hold on, I will get you out!"

I was using my telepathy on him and learned that he was very relieved that I had magically reappeared.

He then pulled the seatback forward, and removed the speaker box that was blocking my way out.

I crawled up and around to see my dad's smiling face. He picked me up and gave me a super, loving hug!

On the ride home, I sat on my dad's lap and purred. I was still reading his mind and he had already figured out that someone must have scared me under the seat.

Then he said to me that he was sorry for not realizing I might be scared in this unfamiliar place with all its strange noises. "Next time, I will park away from all the danger and noise, okay?"

I was relieved and thought that this was a good idea.

This was the moment that I realized city life just wasn't for me! I needed the peace and quiet of the forest and the trees for a safe place to hide.

Chapter Fourteen
PROOF OF TELEPATHY

While we were driving home from the store, big dad surprisingly thanked me for coming with him and watching the truck.

He was still thinking about the scare that I just gave him, hiding under the seat and the time that I had disappeared all night.

My dad realized that he'd better start taking more pictures, in case something tragic were to happen to me.

He never took any pictures of his other cats, and was very sad he hadn't recorded their lives. Big dad decided that he was going to start taking extra pictures of me tomorrow! I was excited and couldn't wait to pose.

Then I did something that really surprised my dad.

Just before he started slowing down to turn onto our dirt road, I stood up instinctively knowing this is where we lived.

He had slowed down and had made many turns on the way home, but I only stood up when we reached our road.

Big dad just couldn't believe that I knew we were almost home. He truly thought that I must have read his mind with my telepathy.

Of course, I had!

After we got home, I read my dad's mind again. He was thinking that he wanted to test my telepathic abilities, so he asked me if I wanted to go for a walk.

Then he thought about this small group of trees located between the garage and horse shed. He was thinking, "Let's walk directly through the middle of these trees on our way up to the cabin at the end of our driveway."

So I obliged and led him exactly the way he had pictured it in his mind. Big dad was impressed!

When we got close to the cabin, my dad started thinking about this huge tree that guarded the right side of our driveway.

I read his mind again, and within thirty seconds I sprinted up this big tree. He was happily surprised and started thinking that I should climb up all the way to the top. So I did!

When I came down, he was thinking that I should come over to the north side of this tree and jump down onto his back.

So once again, I did!

He was very impressed with my abilities and said to me, "You really are a royal psychic super cat!"

After jumping onto his shoulders, I rubbed up against his head, letting my dad know that I love him before finding a comfortable spot to rest.

Then I rode around on big dad's shoulders until he walked back down the driveway to the house. I like doing this because I can see and hunt really good from this elevated position. I also love the free ride!

When we got by the front door my dad must have read my mind and knew I wanted down. He instinctively leaned back and held out his right knee, just like I was thinking!

After getting down safely with the knee trick, I rubbed up against his leg in appreciation.

It was getting close to dinner time so we headed inside to get a snack. When we got into the kitchen, my dad put three gravy snack pouches in front of me by my feeding bowls.

He knew that my favorite flavor was smoked salmon, so he put that one in the middle. Then he thought to himself, "This is the one I want you to pick."

I easily read his mind and put my paw on the pouch in the middle.

Once again, he seemed surprised by my ability. When he opened up the snack that I had picked, he commented to me that I was a very smart cat!

The smoked salmon was delicious, and after dinner, I jumped up into my dad's lap to thank him.

The next morning during our walk, I sensed that big dad wanted to take my picture. I read his mind and knew that he did, so I quickly took a place by a rock and posed for a photograph.

He got his phone ready and after kneeling down, he zoomed in on me before snapping the picture. I wasn't afraid and stood still until he had taken my photo.

After taking this picture of me, my dad realized that I was photogenic because the picture came out like it was taken by a professional.

From this point on, anytime big dad wanted to take my picture, I obliged and posed naturally. During our morning walk, dad took several pictures of me out in the forest. In the evening hours when we were both lounging around the house, I noticed my dad lying on the floor in the living room. He was very still and quiet, so I snuck across the carpet and stood on top of his chest and stomach.

His body was warm and his stomach was soft so I slowly started to knead his belly before I lay down to relax.

This woke him up immediately, and he said to me, "Take it easy Lucky- Son-Jones. Your claws are sharp!"

After getting myself comfortable on top of my dad's stomach, I fell asleep as we both lay there motionlessly.

Chapter Fifteen
THE CAT, THE BAT, AND THE SNAKE

Today when my dad opened up the front door, we both noticed that it was lightly raining outside.

He didn't think that I wanted to go out in the rain, so he started to close the door. He was completely wrong. I *did* want to go outside!

If it was pouring down rain I wouldn't have wanted to go out, but a little mist didn't bother me at all.

I meowed at big dad telling him I wanted out!

In fact, the only time I didn't want to go out for a walk was when it was raining cats and dogs or if there was a foot of snow or more on the ground.

Otherwise, I needed to be on patrol. I sat by the door until dad grabbed his raincoat. He told me I was a crazy cat as we headed out the front door.

I didn't mind a little rain on my fur because I knew when we got home, it would make cleaning my coat a breeze!

After roaming around in the rain for about an hour, I was excited about getting home. I was now soaked, and it felt like I had taken a shower instead of a bath.

Wet fur is easy to groom, so when we got inside I began the

meticulous chore of cleaning myself. When I was done my fur was clean, very soft, and luxurious-looking.

I take pride in keeping myself clean, and after drying off I headed towards the down comforter on my dad's bed.

Amazingly, big dad was already laying down taking himself a little nap!

I kneaded a comfortable spot right next to him before I lay down to absorb his body heat.

He was extremely warm and after listening to his heartbeat, I fell asleep.

Hours later when I woke up, I found myself curled up next to my dad and was surprised that he was holding one of my paws in his hand.

I felt so loved and warm that I did not want to move!

On this rainy day, we had spent the entire afternoon napping together. This was something that I wasn't used to, but I enjoyed it immensely!

While I was laying there I could hear that the rain had stopped, so I slowly started to stretch out to wake myself up. Big dad got up shortly after I did and came into the kitchen where I was comfortably waiting for him on my cardboard cat scratcher.

After dinner, big dad asked me if I wanted to go for a walk. I meowed back. "I sure do!"

After we got outside, I noticed that the pine trees smelled really good.

The aroma they were emitting after the rainstorm was intense, and the whole forest smelled like fresh pine.

The ground was still damp as I headed towards the back of our house.

Immediately, I picked up the scent of a squirrel. I tracked it down when I prowled around these fallen aspen trees, near our backyard fence.

This squirrel was trying to hide under these aspens, and as soon as I got close it bolted over the fence and up the nearest tree.

I just missed catching this elusive varmint and after it disappeared, I sniffed around these fallen trees to remember what these squirrels smelled like.

This varmint's scent was very strong because the rain had washed away most of the other smells in the area.

I recognized its smell and soon realized that this same squirrel had been inside my cat fort, stealing my food!

Then, after searching intensely and absorbing the fresh scent of this squirrel, I looked up and all around.

My dad was nowhere to be found.

I did not know it then, but I soon learned that my dad had gone to hide on me!

I quickly picked up his scent and followed it down the ridge behind our house. When I came to a small rock outcropping, his scent seemed to be everywhere, but he was nowhere to be found.

I searched and prowled, looking for my missing dad.

After inspecting the entire rock formation, I still had not located him.

He apparently had doubled back to fool me!

I then picked up a strong scent heading away from these rocks down towards a group of Aspen trees.

I headed in this direction, trying to track his scent to where he was. His smell was strong, so I knew he must be close.

I stopped, looked, and listened when I approached the Aspen grove. I could hear my dad breathing, but I could not see him. I slowly headed towards these breathing sounds and soon located my dad hiding behind an aspen tree stump.

He was laying down on the ground trying to hide from me. As soon as I found him, he jumped up and tried to scare me.

I wasn't surprised, and after I read his mind, I found out that he had purposely gone to hide on me, to see if I could track him down.

He had noticed that I wasn't paying attention to him when I was sniffing around looking for that squirrel, so he went and hid.

I had no problem tracking him down. That's when I decided I wasn't going to let him do that to me, ever again!

After this hiding incident, I never took my eyes off my big dad when we were out in the forest, even if I was busy hunting.

He was never going to be able to sneak off and hide in the forest on me again.

I was surprised that he had tested my tracking abilities but pleased that I passed with flying colors.

It was starting to get dark now, so we headed back towards the house. I wasn't having any luck hunting tonight, but that all changed when I got back near the garage.

I was searching around the front yard when I heard something fly by, just above my head! I wasn't sure what this noise was, but the next time I heard it coming my way I leaped up three and a half feet into the darkness, thinking I was catching a bird. When I came down, I realized that it was something completely different!

I headed to the front porch, to show my dad what I had just caught.

He was sitting there drinking a beer when I came up to him and dropped this funny-looking and weird-sounding bird at his feet!

He stood up and was absolutely amazed at what he was seeing.

I read my dad's mind. He was thinking, this is no bird, it is a big black bat!

Dad said, "My super cat just leaped up into the nighttime darkness, and somehow caught a bat flying aimlessly above him."

I still wanted to play with this catch, but dad knew it was a bat, so he took it away from me for fear it might have rabies.

After dad disposed of this big flying varmint, he sat there on the front porch thinking to himself, "Is there anything that this cat can't catch?"

It was truly amazing to him, that I could catch a bat!

Dad thought, "No varmint is safe with Lucky-Son-Jones on patrol. He truly is an amazingly talented hunter. Now, he is a Colorado bat cat!"

After I learned that my dad was so proud of me, I snuck back into the darkness to see what else I could find.

* * *

The very next morning, after our morning walk in paradise, I was on patrol in the front yard. My dad was talking on the phone when I saw something moving in the grass to the right of the front porch.

It was traveling at a steady pace, so I went to investigate. When I got close, this stick-like object quickly stopped.

I saw it moving, and was very curious as to what this varmint was. I put my left paw across its back to see what it would do.

Then, as quickly as it stopped it started moving again. It was trying to move away from me, so I put my other paw on top of it to try to slow it down.

That didn't work either, and it kept trying to get away!

Now I was very curious, so I jumped in front of this moving, slithering, stick-like varmint, to try and stop it.

It kept moving forward and slithered right between my legs and under my body.

In fear, I jump straight up into the air to see what this crazy varmint was doing. When I came down, I grasped this stick-like varmint up into my mouth and headed towards my dad sitting on the front porch.

As I carried it heading towards my dad, the stick's body went limp and just hung out of my mouth.

When my dad saw me coming, he jumped up in amazement and said to me, "What have you caught for me now?"

He stood there in absolute disbelief that I was heading towards him with a snake in my mouth!

When I dropped my catch at his feet, he realized that I had caught a medium-sized garden snake.

Then, he said to me, "You crazy cat. You just caught a snake! If you eat this varmint, you really will have snake blood in you!"

I wasn't really interested in eating this slithering, slimy snake. I just wanted to catch it.

As I watched this snake move away back to where freedom

lurked, I heard my dad say to me, "Lucky-Son-Jones, you are the craziest cat west of the Mississippi River! I can't believe that you caught a bat last night and then you bring home a snake today. What a snake-dog, bat-cat! You truly are my Royal Psychic Super Cat."

I was elated that my big dad thought so highly of me in my hunting skills.

This summer has been good to me and I have truly enjoyed all the exploring I have gotten to do, alongside my mountain man dad.

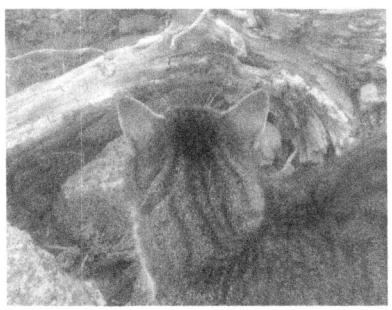

Chapter Sixteen
BIG DOGS

The following morning when we were going outside for a walk, the phone rang just as we were headed out the front door. I continued out and my dad went back inside to answer the phone.

As I stood on the front porch stretching, I looked around for something to catch.

It was a beautiful late summer morning with a slight breeze blowing that would have been perfect, except our closest neighbor had their generator running again.

I am really getting annoyed by this daily irritating and constant buzzing sound that hurts my ears!

As I ventured across the driveway towards the horse shed, I was relieved when this unwanted generator noise suddenly stopped.

Then, because my ears were still ringing, I was caught off guard when danger rushed over the horizon!

I was out in the open between the house and the horse shed, when all of a sudden these two big dogs appeared out of nowhere.

There were no trees close by so I stayed still like a rabbit, hoping these running dogs wouldn't see me.

As they were coming down the hill towards me, one of the dogs stopped by the garage to pee and the other one was heading straight at me!

I no longer felt safe crouching, so I stood up and arched my back to appear larger than usual. I knew running wouldn't help, so I stood my ground and prepared to defend myself.

This approaching dog was big, so I started to hiss and growl, hoping I could thwart its attack!

I wasn't sure that this was an aggressive dog, so when it stuck its head in close to my body, I struck like lightning and walloped its nose with my razor-sharp claws!

Well, this dog let out a yelp so loud, it stopped the other dog from coming any closer.

This big, yelping dog realized that I was a big Colorado mountain cat and a serious force to be reckoned with.

Then, all of a sudden my dad came exploding out the front door at full speed and went running after these two fleeing dogs. He chased them back towards our neighbor's house with the generator.

After he scared them away, he came over to where I was and asked me if I was alright.

I meowed back, "Yes, I had it covered!"

He said that he was sorry he didn't have my back sooner and that I looked huge, with my fur and tail all puffed up.

After the scare and adrenaline rush subsided, we went out for a morning walk in paradise.

As we were walking along, my dad said that he was impressed with my fearless behavior. I had a little strut in my step and felt proud for being brave and standing my ground.

About halfway through this meadow that we were walking in, I spotted a rabbit. I prowled in close, but as soon as it realized I was there, it bolted away with impressive speed.

We were southeast of the house and heading through a meadow towards the dirt road that we lived off of when I heard voices. I look at my dad before I went to investigate.

When we reached the top of the hill, we could see two people walking a dog. It was our neighbors, the Kellys, out for a Sunday walk.

They couldn't see us because they were heading down the road and we were up above them. I could see that they too, owned a big dog.

As I sat there and watched them disappear around the corner, I thought to myself, "It is weird that I have seen three dogs this morning! I haven't seen any dogs since I moved here."

* * *

A few weeks later when big dad and I were out exploring in the Pike National Forest, I had another intense dog scare!

We were hiking along when I heard something coming my way at a very fast pace.

As soon as I saw that it was a big dog, I raced up the nearest tree for safety.

This dog looked hungry and kept whining and barking as it tried to climb the tree I was in.

My dad was fruitlessly trying to scare this dog away, but it would not listen. The dog had a funny-looking device around its neck and seemed very determined to climb up the tree I was hiding in.

I was frightened by this stout dog's aggression, and even more so when a second big dog appeared!

Now I had two big dogs with funny-looking collars, barking at me from the base of this large tree.

Where did these dogs come from and why are they angry with me?

My dad was pissed and started yelling at these two dogs to go home. Soon afterward, their owners magically appeared to control their barking dogs.

After having a conversation with these two men, my dad found out that they were hunting mountain lions with radio-controlled dogs.

The only problem was, they had tracked, hunted, and treed the wrong kind of Mountain cat. Me!

Big dad and I were glad when these men and their noisy dogs disappeared back into the forest.

A short while later, I found the courage to come down out of the big pine tree that protected me. Now I was a little on edge as we continued on our morning walk!

My dad was proud of me for being alert and escaping the danger. On the way home, I read his mind and learned that he wasn't too happy about these two cowardly characters, hunting mountain lions with dogs and scaring the daylights out of me.

These dogs had tried to interrupt our walk in paradise but I wasn't going to let that happen, as I continued to hunt and lead the way.

A short while later, we came to a grove of Aspen trees, camouflaged by really tall and massive pine trees. The leaves on the aspens were starting to change colors and were quite impressive-looking.

We had been out in the forest for a couple hours, and I was starting to get hungry so I stopped so we could get a snack.

After getting something to eat, I continued through the grove of colorful Aspen trees and into an open meadow.

This field had tall grasses growing throughout and took us back in a direction towards the house.

As we traveled downwards into this jungle of grass with the sun on our backs, I was startled by a quick-moving shadow overtaking me.

It was a big red-tailed hawk, who had just silently taken off from that grove of aspen trees that we had just gone through.

I recognized the near-silent swooping sound of these big birds as it soared by, through the thin mountain air.

I was extremely glad big dad was right behind me because his presence surely thwarted any kind of an attack.

As this hawk flew overhead about thirty feet above, it looked straight down at me! After we made eye contact, I watched intensely as this big bird flew gracefully by.

I sensed that this big and mighty hawk was thinking, "You're a lucky cat because if your dad wasn't there, you would have been my next dinner!"

Apparently, dad and I had interrupted this large bird's hunting session by walking into this meadow.

I am completely aware of the danger that these silent predators present, and was extremely glad that my dad was with me!

A short while later, when we came to the lower edge of this meadow that we were traveling through, I heard something moving up ahead.

I immediately jumped up three feet into the air and forward another four. While I was airborne, I could hear exactly where this varmint was.

As soon as I landed, I pounced twice towards the sounds I just heard. After the third jump, I landed with precision right on top of a fat field mouse.

I grasped it up and headed toward the edge of the forest to play.

My dad commented to me that my explosive aerial attack looked awesome! Then he said, "Lucky-Son-Jones, where did you learn how to hunt like that? You must be a Royal, Psychic, Flying Super Cat!"

I thought to myself, "Well, yes I am!"

After playing with this mouse for a while, I picked it up and dropped it at my dad's feet. Lately, I have been trying to repay my dad for the love and time that he spends with me every day by sharing fifty percent of my catches with him.

He genuinely seems impressed by my acts of kindness by accepting and appreciating my donations.

I love my big dad!

I was feeling tired after all this excitement, so I headed back towards the house for a nap.

The next few weeks were uneventful, with no sign of any more stray dogs. I was happy about this but kept on full alert, just in case!

Today my dad asked me if I wanted to go with him to visit with a friend, named Jim. I thought, "Why not? I've never met him."

After traveling a short distance in the Toyota truck, we came to a bumpy dirt road that my dad turned onto.

A short while later, we reached Jim's house. He lived in a small A-frame that had a large side porch. He built a garage next to his house, made out of different diameter cut logs cemented on top of each other to make the walls.

When dad opened up the truck's door, he told me to stay because Jim's big golden retriever was coming up to the truck to say hello!

Jim's old hound dog, Sandy, was friendly and almost blind. Nevertheless, he could always recognize who you were by smell.

After Sandy happily greeted big dad by the open truck door, this huge dog walked right up to the truck and stuck its head in the doorway.

I heard my dad quickly tell Sandy, "Be careful, you big crazy dog. My cat is afraid of dogs and might attack!"

I would have been terrified, but I had already read my dad's mind that this dog was old and blind. I sensed that this big dog was only curious and just wanted to meet me.

This is what happened next!

I was resting on the driver's side floorboard when Sandy stuck his big head in. Instead of attacking with an open claw, I greeted him with a kiss.

After we touched noses, my dad commented to me that he couldn't believe what his eyes had just seen.

He thought, how could it be possible that I wasn't upset about this big dog invading my space? There should have been some hissing and growling going on, with a full-fledged cat attack!

Big dad was impressed that we didn't fight and told me that he would be right back. After he closed the truck's door I jumped up onto the seat to see where my dad was going.

After dad disappeared inside Jim's house, I stood in the open window to see what was going on. I noticed Sandy was close by, and seemed to be keeping an eye on me.

I looked and searched for anything to move, while I enjoyed all the new and interesting smells emanating from this new and unexplored property.

Soon afterward, my dad reappeared and told me I was a good cat for waiting for him.

On the drive home, big dad said to me that he just couldn't believe that Sandy and I had become friends! I used my telepathy on him and learned that he thought this was truly amazing and was happy that we did not fight!

The entire ride home, my dad thought about how much he loves me. He also thought about our special connection to each other and the joy that he feels in his heart every day, spending time with me out in the wilderness.

The joy is mutual, and because of my dad, I have learned to be a talented hunter and a gifted climber. I have become a super-strong Colorado mountain cat, who loves to climb trees, rocks and anything else that stands in my way.

To be valued immensely and loved greatly is the best gift that any animal can receive!

Chapter Seventeen
BUENA VISTA

Today, the month of October has arrived with its cooler temperatures and changing colors. The month of September just flew by for me.

I had a great and endless summer roaming around the forest, exploring! My rock climbing and hunting abilities have surpassed my wildest dreams.

I have become a big, strong cat, with a thirst for adventure. My dad has made all my dreams come true and more.

This morning after our morning walk, I felt like there was something going on, so I used my telepathy on my big dad to see what was up.

I did not realize it till after I read his mind that this coming weekend was our first anniversary. We have been together for almost a year! I am truly happy to be my dad's cat.

In celebration of our one year anniversary, he is taking me back to Buena Vista, Colorado, my birthplace, to go camping!

A friend of his, named Eddie, is going to come up from Denver and meet us there.

I was psyched to learn this and couldn't wait to go camping again.

The weekend came quickly, and I was excited to go back to the forest that I had escaped to when I was younger.

When Friday evening came along, we watched the weather and they said that it was going to be a sunny and beautiful weekend.

After dinner, I watched my dad load up the back of the truck with all the camping supplies. He is so organized that I'm sure he won't forget anything.

The dawn came quickly and I was so excited about going camping, that I shortened our morning walk together.

It was early when we left the house in the Toyota truck. I took my usual spot on my dad's lap, so I could stick my head out the window.

The sun was coming up and the morning air was chilly. After we drove out to the tar road, I found a comfortable spot next to my dad. I knew the ride to Buena Vista was just over an hour, so I decided to take a nap.

It wasn't long before dad said to me that we are almost there. We had just driven over Trout Creek Pass at an elevation of 10,200 feet above sea level and now were descending down towards the small mountain town of Buena Vista, Colorado.

This tiny little town sat at an elevation of 8000 feet above sea level and was located in a valley between two mountain ranges.

The Collegiate Peaks mountain range rose to an elevation of 14,000 plus feet and sat to the west of Buena Vista. To the east was Trout Creek Pass.

This mountain valley was fairly flat and had impressive views in all directions!

When we entered this cozy little town, I stood up to see where we were. We were supposed to meet Eddie at the local gas station at eight a.m. before heading into the San Isabel National Forest to camp.

Eddie was waiting for us when we arrived, and after dad and him had a short conversation, we raced off to find a great campsite.

After entering the forest near Buena Vista, we had to go extremely slow because the dirt road was washed out and really bumpy.

I took my usual spot on my dad's lap to get the best view. The forest was lush and smelled really fresh and pine-like. After traveling for a while, we came to the top of a rocky ridge. We were now several miles east of town at an elevation of 10,000 feet.

When big dad stopped the truck and opened up the door, I immediately jumped out to investigate. The view was absolutely breathtaking!

We were in a flat camping spot on top of a ridge that had two boulder piles on either side. I was extremely excited about rock climbing and going exploring.

I could see the small town of Buena Vista way down below us. Across the valley and to the west stood Mt. Princeton, a 14,200-foot massive peak, that rose 6,000 feet above this tiny town.

The Collegiate Peaks mountain range was over 100 miles long and consisted of ten different 14,000-plus foot peaks in a row, named after colleges around the country.

I was a little frightened as I watched Eddie get out of his truck. My dad introduced me to his longtime friend and told me that he likes cats. This did make me feel better.

Eddie was the same age as my dad and was excited to get out of the big city to do some camping with us.

I wasn't interested in socializing because I had two large boulder piles to explore.

After convincing my dad to take me for a walk, we headed

towards the left side of the campsite to explore the 300-foot high mountain of boulders that was the highest point on the ridge.

It was easy hiking, and after I led the way I looked back to see Eddie and my dad following me.

There were big pine trees everywhere that camouflaged the hillside. They looked enticing, so I raced up one to sharpen my claws.

I was so excited and pumped up, that I climbed forty feet up into this tree. The view was outstanding as I searched around for a varmint to catch.

I could hear my dad and Eddie talking as they passed under the tree that I was in.

I didn't want them to beat me to the top, so I navigated my way down out of this tree and exploded past them to take the lead.

It did not take us long to reach the summit. The view was impressive, and all we could see were massive mountains protruding up everywhere!

It was a spectacular sight, looking at these treeless peaks that jutted up out of nowhere and were frosted with snow.

After hanging out for a while at the top of these rocks, I read my dad's mind that he wanted to head down and set up the tent and get things ready for the campfire tonight.

When we got back, I prowled around the perimeter of the campsite while Eddie and my dad set up their tents.

I quickly discovered a ground squirrel living close by. I saw it disappear into a hole in the ground, so I went to investigate. After sniffing around for a couple of minutes, I noticed the same ground squirrel watching me. It came out of another hole about fifteen feet away. I immediately raced after it when it took off running in the other direction.

It quickly disappeared into another hole and wouldn't come out to play.

It was a beautiful sunny day, and I was enjoying myself exploring around this new campsite. Eventually, I searched around the entire camp spot and ended up close to where Eddie had set up his tent.

He had placed his old canvas tent on the left side of the campsite, directly under a big tree and over a soft bed of pine needles.

He is a true Boy Scout, and I was impressed that he was going to sleep on the ground! After checking out Eddie's tent fort, I headed over to investigate what my dad had accomplished.

He had set up his tent on the right side of the camp, next to a rock ledge that stood up about three feet and ran parallel to the truck.

The fire pit was located in the middle of the campsite, about sixty feet from either tent.

After they had the camp set up, I followed them both around while they collected wood for the fire tonight.

I was watching Eddie as he picked up a log, and immediately I saw a field mouse trying to escape in the opposite direction.

I crouched down and leaped four feet through the air, right on top of this unsuspecting mouse.

After catching it, I ran to a nearby meadow to play.

This was a fast little varmint and a tasty, well-deserved snack that I enjoyed for lunch!

When my dad and Eddie finished setting up the camp, I convinced them to take me for another walk towards the other rock hill located to the right of our campsite.

I led the way, and my dad and Eddie followed! After traversing 200 yards along the top of the ridge, we came to the other boulder pile.

This one wasn't as high up as the other and didn't have as many trees to climb on. I felt bold and fired up taking us to the top.

When we got near the summit, I overheard Eddie commenting to my dad that he thought I looked like a dog, leading the way.

Eddie did not know that I was a royal, psychic, flying super cat who always led the way!

The view was still spectacular as we reach the top. Within

seconds of being there, I noticed something moving down below us on the other side of this hill.

My dad saw it too and commented that there was a herd of bighorn sheep trying to stay camouflaged among the rocks.

Amazingly, their fur coats were the same color as the rocks that were hiding them.

The dominant male in the herd turned his head when he heard us moving above him. I don't think we would have noticed them standing there if he had stayed still.

The herd must have sensed danger because they slowly started moving away from us.

As we sat at the top enjoying the great view, we could see the entire herd of bighorn sheep slowly disappearing over the ridge.

Eddie said that we were lucky to see them because they are masters at keeping themselves hidden.

I decided to prowl that way to see if I could track them down!

We soon came to the spot where they were hiding, so I sniffed around to become familiar with their smell. Then, I followed their scent and tracked them down.

By the time I got to the top of the ridge where we had last seen them, the whole herd had somehow vanished into thin air!

Speaking of thin air, I heard Eddie say to my dad that he needed to take a break to catch his breath. He was having difficulties breathing at 10,000 feet above sea level.

I was in great shape, and personally, I didn't notice the elevation.

After resting a while, we continued hiking along the top of the ridge heading north away from the campsite. I was having a blast exploring this new terrain, and even more so that I was allowed to lead the way.

Eddie seemed to be really enjoying himself, and I was impressed that he and my dad were keeping up to my fast pace.

After looking down the ridge that we had just traveled up, I noticed that the campsite was no longer visible. We had hiked over a mile through the San Isabel National Forest and were now at the end of this ridge.

Everything sloped down from here, so I decided to head east away from these descending meadows towards higher ground.

Up ahead, I could see a rocky outcropping. There were hundreds of boulders scattered around, almost as if there had been an explosion!

The trees of the forest were thinning out and weren't as abundant as they were down by the campsite. The grassy sloping meadows at this elevation seemed to be endless and rolled along as far as the eye could see.

When I reached the boulders of this elevated rock outcropping, I smelled the scent of a rabbit.

My dad and Eddie were trailing behind, so I knew I had a couple of minutes of quiet hunting time before they arrived! I immediately went on patrol to see if I could locate it. This rabbit's scent was getting stronger as I navigated my way around these three-foot diameter boulders.

The mountain meadow grasses had grown in tall around these fallen rocks, almost completely camouflaging them.

After sneaking around several of the boulders, I came to a small hole that went under one of them. This varmint's scent was strong as I sniffed around.

The rabbit had made its home in a secure spot, completely hidden by the rocks and tall mountain meadow grasses.

Pretty smart!

I was impressed with this rabbit's ability to find such a stealth location to live.

I found a comfortable spot near the entrance to its hole, hoping it would want to come out and play.

A few minutes later I heard my dad calling for me. Apparently, he couldn't see me hiding among the rocks, so I stayed stealthy and hidden!

When I heard my dad and Eddie getting close, I crouched down and prepared to launch myself from a standstill. I was planning on jumping up three feet through the tall mountain grasses to the top of Mr. Rabbit's rock, to surprise them.

Then, with lightning speed, I did just that. I silently leaped out of nowhere up to the top of this rock, surprising them both!

I heard my dad say to me, "You crazy cat. I was wondering where you were."

I was pretty proud of myself for scaring them, so I started strutting my stuff around the top of this Colorado mountain boulder.

I heard Eddie say to my dad that he was impressed with my fearless ability to lead the way!

Then, big dad told Eddie that he thinks that I might have been a dog in my last life because I act more like a dog than a cat.

I read my dad's mind and learned that he couldn't believe it was possible for a cat to be brave enough to go out exploring with his dad in the Colorado wilderness. He was truly amazed at my need for adventure and my thirst to climb trees, rocks, and mountains.

As I led the way, Eddie listened intently as my dad told him story after story of my unique abilities.

When I reached the top of the rolling mountain meadow that we were traveling through, I could see a dirt road winding away over the horizon.

This was the road that we had driven up on, that kept going east through the forest, away from our campsite.

I decided to head this way and take the forest road back to the campsite.

When we all reached the dirt road and were heading in that direction, I heard Eddie say to my dad, "How does Lucky know to go this way to get us back to camp?"

Big dad replied, "This is proof of Lucky's telepathy, because how else would he know how to get us back to the camp spot when we are over a mile away. I am sure he can read my mind because he always knows which way to go to get us home or back to the campsite.

"Sometimes I am surprised by his abilities. Like the time I told you about how Lucky had led us through the forest in the dark, over three-quarters of a mile back to the truck in the area we had never been to before. That was simply amazing because I wasn't even sure how to get us back!"

I was very happy that my dad thought so highly of me and felt overly excited about the adventure we had just taken.

As I trotted along down this rolling forest road, I heard my dad whispering something to Eddie. I couldn't hear exactly what he said because there was too much ground noise caused by their walking.

I read big dad's mind and learned that he had whispered to Eddie that he was going to test my telepathy, to prove to him that I did in fact, possess these special abilities.

There were two trees up ahead, one on the left side and one on the right. Both trees were out in the middle of a meadow about fifty feet from the road and were the only ones close by.

Then, my dad whispered to Eddie, "Watch and you will see. He can read my mind!"

Big dad was thinking, "Lucky I want you to climb up the tree on the right side of the road."

Even though this tree was kind of out of the way, I was proud of my ability, so I went over there and sprinted up to the top.

Eddie was absolutely impressed and said to my dad that he was very lucky to find and adopt me.

After he said that, I thought to myself, "I am truly the lucky one. I have the greatest dad in the world who loves me dearly!"

When I climbed down out of that tree and onto my dad's shoulders, I could sense how proud he was of me! He told me I was a good boy for showing Eddie the truth about me being a Royal Psychic Flying Super Cat.

I rubbed up against his head to tell him that I love him. Then, I found a comfortable spot on his right shoulder and laid down for the free ride back to the campsite.

When I saw the blue truck and tent up ahead, I got excited and wanted down. My dad sensed that I did, leaned back, and put his right knee out so I could jump down safely.

I ran ahead towards the truck, hoping that some varmint might be sneaking around the camp spot, trespassing.

It was a beautiful sunny fall day and I had a blast exploring with my dad and his friend Eddie. We had all worked up a good appetite, so dinner got started early

Big dad gave me a scrumptious tuna gravy snack that I wolfed down immediately. They were having cheeseburgers in paradise, cooked on Eddie's small, portable barbecue.

After dinner, I sat close by and cleaned my chops. The sun was starting to disappear over the horizon, and I noticed the air temperature dropping quickly.

It was going to be a cool fall night out here in the forest of Buena Vista Colorado!

I found a comfortable spot to rest while I watched Eddie and my dad build a campfire.

The sunset was intense as the daylight faded over the massive and extremely high peaks of the Continental Divide.

It soon got dark and I was in my glory laying closeby watching the flames of the campfire roar up to over seven feet above the firepit. These large flames were frightening to me, but the heat radiating from them felt really good in the cool, crisp mountain air.

There was a crescent moon visible tonight, and when it disappeared over the horizon, I noticed the nighttime air temperature had already dropped to thirty-two degrees Fahrenheit in the campsite.

Chapter Eighteen
THE GROWL

It wasn't long after the moon had vanished that my dad and Eddie decided it was time to hit the hay, so they headed towards their tents.

The temperature was below freezing as I jumped up into the back of the truck. Everything felt cold as I tried to find a comfortable spot to sleep. I was glad when big dad settled into his sleeping bag! He was very warm, so I snuggled in close.

After getting a kiss on the head and being told that my dad loves me, I rolled up into a ball to become toasty warm. I buried my head and ears next to my dad's body and then puffed up my fur to help keep me extra warm.

A few hours later, I was woken up by the frigid air temperature looming inside the back of the Toyota truck!

It was downright freezing, and I was cold even though I was right next to my dad.

I quickly thought up this idea to climb inside my dad's sleeping bag to warm myself up.

In the darkness, I located the entrance to his sleeping bag by the sound of his breathing. When I got myself close, big dad must have sensed that I was there because he magically opened up his covers and asked me if I wanted to come in to get warm.

I couldn't believe that he had read my mind, even while he was sleeping!

I did not hesitate to head inside and pull off the winter coat maneuver. Big dad was laying on his right side with his knees slightly bent. I crawled into his sleeping bag in the pitch-black of the night until I reached his folded knees. Then I turned around so that my back was right next to his warm belly.

My dad was incredibly toasty and the heat radiating off his body was intense. It did not take long to warm up my frozen body.

While I lay there comfortably resting, I thought about how special my dad really is!

It was unbelievable to me that my dad had sensed that I was cold, and allowed me to come inside his sleeping bag to get warmed up.

What a warm and thoughtful big dad I have.

When I was laying there getting toasty, my dad stroked my back and said to me, "Lucky, you're a super-smart cat."

After about twenty-five minutes had passed, I became overly toasty and wanted out! Again, my dad sensed that I did, and opened up his sleeping bag. I had gotten uncomfortably hot laying there next to him.

I managed to fall asleep for another three hours before I got cold and wanted back inside.

My dad magically knew I was cold and opened up his warm enclosure right as I approached the entrance. I quickly went inside and pulled off the new sleeping bag maneuver!

My dad was happy to let me do this several more times before the sun came up. Both dad and I procrastinated to get up early and go for a walk.

After I did, I sat in the sun by the screen of the tent door to stay warm and waited for big dad to get up.

I breathed in the cold, fresh mountain air while I looked across the campsite and remembered that my dad's friend, Eddie, was camping with us.

His tent was still in the shade, and it appeared very cold over there!

Then I started hearing a disturbing noise that I had never heard before. It was emanating from his direction, and sounded so strange that it started to scare me!

I wasn't sure what to do, so I started growling, hoping I could scare away whatever it was that was making this weird noise.

This was the first time that I had ever growled, so I growled louder in an attempt to sound bigger. Unfortunately, that wasn't working because the noise was getting louder and more frequent.

Then I heard my dad say to me, "What are you growling at, Lucky-Son-Jones?"

I wasn't sure, but I felt the need to make some growling noise.

Big dad got up to see what all the commotion was about. I used my telepathy on him and learned that this strange noise that we were both hearing was Eddie snoring!

I was completely relieved to know this because I did not know what this strange noise was. My dad was relieved to know that his friend, Eddie, hadn't frozen to death during the frigid night.

According to the thermometer, it had managed to get down to twenty degrees Fahrenheit last night.

My dad smartly heated up one of my gravy pouches in the water he had boiled for his tea. This delicious snack tasted extra good all warmed up, and was perfect on such a cold morning.

Thankfully, the sun warmed up the air temperature in the campsite quickly, and after breakfast, I was ready to go for a walk.

The San Isabel National Forest was immense in size, and there was so much we hadn't explored yet, that I felt a little bit anxious as I waited for my dad.

After he unzipped the door to the tent, I hurried outside to see if there were any varmints close by. It was a beautiful, sunny day high in the mountains, even though it was cold.

I headed towards Eddie's tent to see if he had gotten up. I

could hear him still snoring as I searched around for something to move.

A few minutes later, I heard my dad ask Eddie if he was going for a morning walk with us.

He responded and said that he was too sore and tired to go!

After hearing this, I felt amused as I led the way and big dad followed. We headed over the ridge, and through the woods, towards grandma's house we went.

Along the way, I realized that the long journey my dad and I had taken Eddie on yesterday had worn that old city boy out!

We are mountain folk, and hiking in the foothills at this elevation doesn't even bother us. My dad and I are strong and physically fit because we hike around in the forest every day.

I have to thank big dad for that because he has spent the time taking us outside for a walk ever since he adopted me.

I was excited about being outside hiking with my dad, and even more so that he had taken me back to the forest of Buena Vista, where I was born!

The joy I was feeling this morning was intense, and it put more energy in every step as I trotted along.

Shortly after we left the campsite, I heard some funny-sounding noises coming in our direction. I slowed down my approach and soon realized that there was a flock of big birds on the ground, right in front of me.

These birds were making weird noises that sounded like the quack of a duck as they moved slowly through the forest away from us.

I looked back at my dad to read his mind. I learned that these big birds were wild turkeys out on their morning walk. I also discovered that the male turkeys can grow large enough to weigh over one hundred pounds.

I held my position because these birds were too big to chase after.

These turkeys knew that we were close by, but didn't even flinch as they slowly traveled through. It is unbelievable to me

THE GROWL

how many different kinds of creatures live in the safety of the forest.

I felt the need for a hug, so I rubbed up against my dad's leg, and he instinctively picked me up to give me one.

Then after receiving some love, I headed up to his shoulder so I could watch the turkeys disappear.

I have seen some big birds out here in the forest, but these turkeys take the cake!

I rode around on my dad's shoulders for a short period of time, until I felt safe enough to want down. After being put on the ground, I led the way, heading southeast in the direction that we had traveled to get here from our house.

Along the deer trail that I had found, I used my telepathy on my dad and learned that he was having fun exploring with me. He was also entertained at the fact that I was heading in the exact direction a bird would fly to get us home!

A short while later big dad said to me, "Are you taking us home, Lucky-Son-Jones? You crazy cat, it is over fifty miles away, and I'm not walking that far." Then he said to me, "Come on, let's head back to the campsite. I am getting hungry."

I was impressed with my dad for realizing that I did, in fact, know the way back to the house.

I hesitated to turn around, but after I did, I traveled along the edge of the forest that ran parallel to a rolling meadow.

Soon afterwards, I heard a mouse squeak close by in the long grasses of the meadow that we were walking through.

I immediately became airborne, and after leaping up three feet and forward five, I was able to pinpoint exactly where this varmint was. During my brief flight, I was able to see this mouse fleeing and after I landed, I sprang towards this mouse and landed right on top of it.

As I took this varmint out in the meadow to play, I heard my dad say to me, "Lucky-Son-Jones, you really are a flying super cat!"

I was happy that big dad had witnessed my aerial attack on this mouse because this was becoming one of my favorite ways to hunt.

If a squirrel can fly, so can I!

After playing with this big field mouse, I grasped it up and delivered it to my dad's feet. I wanted to share my catch with him in appreciation for taking us camping again.

We were still heading back to camp, but on a slightly different path than we had taken this morning. When the meadow ended and the forest started overtaking us, we came to a hill that had a mini-ridge of rocks scattered up and down and all around.

As we started up this hill, my dad found a good rock to sit on and said that he was taking a break! I thought that this was a good idea because I was thirsty. After getting a drink and a quick snack, I started searching around these colorful rocks while my dad rested.

A couple minutes later, I came to a cave-like opening that was really cool-looking. It had black and grey-striped markings throughout that slanted upwards and went in about seven feet.

When I heard my dad coming, I quickly went in to hide! It was a narrow cave that went in about seven feet before becoming too small to go any further. I had difficulties turning around, so I had to back out until I had room to do so.

My dad was standing outside this cave when I reappeared at the opening. He said to me that I was completely camouflaged by the striped color of this cave, and if it wasn't for the white diamond marking on my chest, he would not have seen me hiding there.

We continued up this hill along this ridge of boulders. They were four to five feet in diameter and scattered around perfectly, so we could travel through them.

Soon, the big boulders started to disappear and the rocks of the mini-ridge became smooth and very colorful.

I led the way and big dad followed. When I raced up these smooth rocks to the top, I came across another cave that went in about fifteen feet. I could see light coming through from the other side, so I went in to investigate.

This cave was wide at its entrance and narrowed down like a funnel at the end where the light was coming from. This small opening was just big enough for a cat to fit through, so I did and disappeared out of sight.

When my dad reached this cave, I was nowhere to be found because I was on the other side, exploring.

He magically knew that I had gone through, and waited for me at the entrance. A few minutes later I stuck my head back into the small opening, where the light was coming from.

Big dad was pleasantly surprised and fully entertained that I had reappeared!

He could sense that I was having fun and patiently waited for me to check everything out.

I knew that we were not far from the campsite, so I took my time exploring before we headed that way.

Eddie was happily waiting for us when we returned. He had cooked up some bacon and eggs, so dad and him sat down to enjoy breakfast together.

After getting a quick snack, I started cleaning myself up and thinking about how much fun I was having camping with my dad and his friend Eddie.

I still can't believe that my dad knows about all these cool camping spots, and even more so that he takes me with him so I can enjoy 'The Great Outdoors.'

After breakfast, I saw my dad get up from his chair and move towards the tent. I seized the moment and jumped up into his pre-warmed foldable camping chair to get really comfy.

Like the old saying goes, "Move your meat, lose your seat!"

I took full advantage of being allowed to rest in my dad's comfortable outdoor chair.

Big dad soon noticed that I had stolen his spot and grabbed the camera, so he could take my picture.

It was another beautiful sunny day in Colorado, and we have been blessed with another great weekend for camping. Around midday, I heard Eddie tell my dad that he had to leave early. He had to work tomorrow and had a three-hour drive to get home.

As I rested in big dad's chair, I watched Eddie take down his tent and pack up all his camping supplies.

I was sad to see my dad's friend leave because I could tell that they were close. He was really friendly and nice towards me and I enjoyed taking him on a journey, through the forest of Buena Vista, Colorado.

After Eddie left, I convinced my dad to take me back to the summit of the boulder pile closest to the campsite.

When we got up to the top, we sat there for a good part of the afternoon, just enjoying each other's company and taking in the grand scenery.

I can't believe that I was born right here in this little town of Buena Vista and never saw these massive mountains.

Later that day big dad told me the bad news that we too, had to pack up and head home.

Then he told me some good news that was music to my ears!

He said that he was planning on taking us to new spots for hiking and camping because he was flat-out tired of listening to that constant, irritating, generator noise coming from our new neighbor's next door!

Meow-who!!

Chapter Nineteen
MY SPECIAL DAD

My big dad loves 'The Great Outdoors' and without a doubt, was born to be a mountain man.

All the free luxuries the wilderness has to offer, including the fantastic views, the clean air, the sunrises, the sunsets, and all the massive protruding mountains, truly makes living in paradise worthwhile. I agree!

I love this man with all my heart. He has changed my life in a very special way with all his love and devotion.

I truly feel that we were meant to be together. The special connection and love that we share are immeasurable, and the time that we spend together is priceless!

Thanks to my dad I have become the leanest, fittest, and strongest cat west of the Mississippi River. I am all muscle and have become one lightning-fast hunter.

I never thought it was possible to have such a close, loving, and meaningful relationship with a man.

The telepathic abilities that we both possess are intense, and I love that we can read each other's minds.

On several occasions he has tested my abilities to do so, just to make sure he wasn't dreaming!

We also have a physical connection to each other. Anytime big dad holds me in his arms, I can feel his positive energy flowing and how much he loves me!

I have never felt this with any other man or woman.

My dad is special and when he hugs me, my fur becomes electrified with static electricity.

Then when he strokes my back, there is a sparkling, crackling sound produced as the static electricity discharges between his hand in my fur.

I love this feeling!

I love our daily walks together!

I love that I get hugs and kisses every day!

I have never felt so loved and valued in all my life. I am so glad that I was adopted by this man. He really loves me and I love him.

Ever since we went camping together, my dad has been giving me a kiss on the head just before we go to sleep.

I love how he treats me and his unique love makes me feel like the luckiest cat west of the Mississippi River!

My dad is so cool that he just came up with a new two-tone whistle that he uses to call me instead of using my name.

The advantage of this whistling is that he can call me without making a lot of noise. I like this because it doesn't scare away any varmints I might be hunting, and it also keeps our stealth location secret to any of our neighbors.

I like how it sounds and I have been responding to it to let him know that I understand what he is doing.

His new two-tone whistling is unique and almost sounds like a bird chirp, rather than a whistle. Crazy dad, I think he might have some bird blood in him.

I have been truly blessed to have had the luck to meet this man. My only hope is that other adopted animals find the same love, that I have found!

So with a kiss on the head, I say farewell to all my friends and readers until my next book, *Through My Cat's Eyes Two, The Adventure Continues*!

THE END

-Lucky-Son-Jones

AFTERWORD

Lucky-Son-Jones, my special cat,
truly is the luckiest cat
west of the Mississippi River.
He is so fun to take for a walk, and the joy that I receive on our
daily adventures is so rewarding, that it always makes my day.
I love this cat.

Check out Lucky's Website
https://luckyswebsite.weebly.com/

ALSO BY TROY JONES

To learn more about the cat who thinks he is a dog, and his newest adventures, read the other two books in the series:

ACKNOWLEDGMENTS

I would like to thank Ed Molloy, Sr., for helping me with retrieving Lucky's pictures from my phone. He is a good friend.

Thank you also to Debbie Allen for help with publishing the book.

And mostly, I would like to thank my special cat for the great memories we share hiking around and hunting in the wilderness of Colorado. This book would not have been possible without Lucky's unique participation and psychic abilities.

ABOUT THE AUTHOR

Troy Jones is an animal lover, who enjoys the outdoors. He lives, works, and plays high in the Colorado Rocky Mountains.

Lucky Son-Jones, the cat who thinks he's a dog, also lives high in the Colorado Rocky Mountains. He is an avid hunter, with a thirst for adventure.

For more information and to see all photos in color:
https://luckyswebsite.weebly.com/
troyjones994@gmail.com

Made in United States
Orlando, FL
12 January 2024